GREAT
WALKS
of
BRITAIN

GREAT WALKS *of* BRITAIN

BTA
British Tourist Authority

Produced specially for the British Tourist Authority
by Ward Lock Limited, Artillery House, Artillery Row,
London SW1P 1RT,
a Cassell company

The walks in this book have previously been published
in the Great Walks series.

Photographs by David Ward (pages 19–117)
and John Heseltine (pages 119–215)

Printed and bound in Spain by Graficromo

ISBN 0 7095 4052 3

Previous page *Rolling hills in the Peak District*

CONTENTS

Contents

INTRODUCTION TO WALKING IN BRITAIN

At the present time walking is by far the most popular outdoor pursuit in Britain; in fact surveys show that it has more than twice as many active participants as the next most popular, swimming. In any month in the summer an incredible ten million adults go for a walk of at least two miles (3.2 km); of these, nearly half a million undertake a fairly serious ramble or hill walk. Surprisingly, perhaps, walking holds its popularity throughout the year and these figures do not drop off very much even in the winter. It appeals to men and women, to all age groups and to people from a wide variety of backgrounds.

Although this popularity is not a recent phenomenon, there has nevertheless been a big increase in enthusiasm for walking over the past 30 years or so. In 1965 the membership of the Ramblers' Association—the most important walkers' organization in Britain—was 13,770; at the end of February 1989, the membership had risen to 68,073, nearly five times greater. There is every likelihood that it will continue to rise in the future.

One attractive feature of walking, and one which plays a big part in its popularity, is the absence of a cost barrier at the beginning; unlike some other activities where expensive equipment has to be bought—or borrowed from trusting friends—before anything can be done. Provided they are sound and comfortable, oldish ordinary clothing and footwear are usually quite sufficient for short lowland walks in good summer weather. It is later, once the bug has bitten and the walker wants to progress to greater things (particularly for walking over mountains and moorlands), that specialized clothing and equipment becomes essential. It is best to seek advice before buying anything, and specialist shops will be only too glad to give it. It is generally a sound policy to buy the best equipment that can be afforded for this should give the longest and most reliable use. As good quality clothing usually wears well, given reasonable care, all purchases should be regarded as long term investments. 'Buy in haste, repent at leisure' is as sound a piece of advice here as in life generally.

Walkers in Britain are fortunate in having available some superb maps, produced by the Ordnance Survey, which have been designed with walking in mind. Pathfinder maps are usually the most useful for they show considerable detail, e.g. fences, hedges, etc., together with, in England and Wales, the paths and ways over which the public has a right to walk. For some areas of particular interest to walkers, such as National Parks, the Ordnance Survey has also produced a special series of Outdoor Leisure maps, which give the same detail but, area for area they are considerably cheaper than the Pathfinder maps. Finally, there is a third series, the Landranger maps, which are very popular and usually satisfactory for mountain and moorland areas; again these show all public paths and ways for England and Wales although, as field boundaries are omitted, they are generally not so good for lowland areas.

The Countryside Commission has recently estimated that there are about 135,000 miles (217,000 km) of paths in England and Wales over which the public has a legal right to walk. Some of these are footpaths reserved for walkers, while others are bridleways which are also open to cyclists and horse riders. Although not evenly distributed over the country—the Lincolnshire fens, for example, have very few—almost all areas have some. In addition, landowners sometimes allow walkers to use certain paths, even though there is no legal right of way; these are known as Permissive Paths. There is almost certainly no walker alive today who has walked all the paths of Britain, even though some seem to be trying hard enough!

The public has access also to some areas of open country, even though there may be no public rights of way across them. For example, most commons near older towns and villages fall into this category, as do public parks and open spaces. In some cases access is allowed through long-established tradition; in others because the owner has given permission—the National Trust are particularly praiseworthy in this respect—or perhaps negotiated an Access Agreement with the local authority. The Peak Park Joint Planning Board, who are responsible for the Peak District National Park, have been most energetic in negotiating these agreements and large areas are now available to walkers because of them.

It is usually agreed that the best walking in England and Wales is to be found in the National Parks. This is not to suggest that excellent walking cannot be found anywhere else. Anyone who has walked in the northern Pennines, in central Wales or in the Cotswolds—none designated as National Parks—will know how ridiculous such a notion is! But, with that proviso, the National Parks do stand out as areas of exceptional beauty. At present, there are ten—or eleven with the Norfolk Broads, where the difference is largely one of name only—created between 1950 and 1957. The Peak District was the first and the

Opposite *May Beck*
in the North York Moors

8

Brecon Beacons the last. It must be emphasized that none of them are 'owned' by the State, almost all the land is still privately owned, as it was before designation.

Each National Park has its own character, and walkers argue endlessly on their relative merits. The Lake District is the largest; a wonderful region of high mountains—including Scafell Pike, the highest in England—and lakes of breathtaking beauty. Some of its mountains, such as Skiddaw and those around Grasmere, are large grassy, whale-backed hills, but the central mountains are splintered peaks with great cliffs and scree and boulder slopes. The smallest National Park is the Pembrokeshire Coast which differs from the others in being split up into three separate parts and consisting largely of low-lying coastland with little wilderness area.

Snowdonia is a harsher region than either, with rock peaks such as Tryfan and Crib-goch where the use of hands as well as feet is the order of the day. It has its lovely valleys and softer hills, too. The traverse of the Snowdon Horseshoe is the finest mountain expedition south of the Scottish Highlands—but suitable only for those who have a good head for heights! Further south the Brecon Beacons National Park, rising to its highest point in Pen y Fan, offers ridge walking of the highest quality. Dartmoor is a lonely area of bare moorland topped by tors of eroded granite, a magic place of hill-forts, barrows and clapper bridges. Its neighbour, Exmoor, is smaller and includes a coastline of high cliffs and attractively wooded combes.

The Peak District, hemmed in by great conurbations around Manchester and Sheffield, has been at the centre of much of the fight for access. In the north, the moors of the Dark Peak offer some of the toughest terrain in England; in the south, the White Peak is by contrast limestone plateau cut into by rivers, such as the Dove and the Wye, which have become bywords for spectacular beauty. The Yorkshire Dales have become world-famous through their association with the books of James Herriot and the television programmes made from them, so that people who have never set foot there are familiar with the water-splash on the road from Swaledale into Arkengarthdale, the vet's house at Askrigg and the old bridge in Langthwaite. The North York Moors is another coastal National Park, but also includes an extensive moorland area, with its highest point on Urra Moor, penetrated by many green dales of considerable beauty. Finally, there is Northumberland, furthest north and least visited of all the Parks, whose boundaries encompass Hadrian's Wall and the Cheviot Hills. Its symbol is the curlew, that wonderful bird of the northern moors whose lovely liquid call is the very breath of early spring.

In addition to the Parks, some regions have been designated as Areas of Outstanding Natural Beauty. The smallest of these is Dedham Vale on the Essex-Suffolk border, which has associations with John Constable, while the largest (only two National Parks are larger) is the North Pennines, a lonely area south of the Wall, which was designated in 1988.

At present there are no National Parks in Scotland (although there are some country or regional parks). This is not, however, an adverse reflection of the beauty of Scotland's countryside. Nobody who has walked in Scotland will doubt that a dozen National Parks could be created there if it was thought appropriate. Scotland has much larger areas of high mountain country than anywhere else in Britain (in total, more than the rest of Britain put together), with many peaks over 3000 ft (914 m)—called Munros after Sir Hugh Thomas Munro who prepared a list of them in 1891—and even some over 4000 ft (1219 m). There is also an added dimension in the large number of islands off the mainland coast, many of which—in particular Skye—give superb walking. Scotland has a much lower density of population than England and Wales, so that, despite the number of visitors, the countryside is on the whole much quieter than it is, for example, in the National Parks. In practice, there are generally no restrictions to wandering in wild areas in Scotland, provided that no damage is caused to the countryside and local practices are observed, although there may not be a legal right.

The most exciting development in the walking world over the past 20 years or so has been the creation of long distance paths. The most important of these, recently renamed National Trails, have been created under the auspices of the Countryside Commission. The first of these—and still the longest—was the Pennine Way, which goes from Edale in the Peak District to Kirk Yetholm over the Scottish border, 250 miles (402 km) of glorious walking, mostly over wild and lonely moorlands. Offa's Dyke Path, named after the great earthwork thrown up by Offa in the eighth century, follows approximately the English-Welsh border; the Cleveland Way goes in a great horseshoe along the boundary of the North York Moors National Park; and the Ridgeway follows a line of chalk downs along the ancient routes of the Wessex Ridgeway and the Icknield Way. Southern England has National Trails along the North and South Downs; eastern England its Peddars Way and Norfolk Coast Path, and in the south-west four separate Trails provide a continuous path around the entire peninsula. Scotland has two superb long distance paths, the West Highland Way which goes from near Glasgow to Fort William and the Southern Upland Way which goes from coast to coast across the south, with work progressing on a third.

The creation of long distance paths, however, is a game that all can play—although to different rules—and organizations such as County and District Councils, Ramblers' Association groups, walking clubs and even individuals, have designed them and published guidebooks so that others may follow. Perhaps the best known of these is the superb Coast to Coast Walk which was created by A. Wainwright, but nowadays there are few areas which are without them. There are so many, in fact, that a National Register of Long Distance Paths has been established so that would-be entrepreneurs can check before starting that they have not been anticipated!

Although most walking is essentially non-competitive, the competitive element has never been entirely absent. The Three Peaks Walk of Yorkshire, on which walkers reach the summits of Pen-y-ghent, Ingleborough and Whernside and return to the starting point within 12 hours, was first completed as long ago as 1887. In the Lake District in 1932, Bob Graham climbed 42 peaks over 2000 ft (610 m) in 24 hours, a feat which involved 72 miles (116 km) of walking and 27,000 ft (8230 m) of climbing! In 1955, Bill Cowley devised the Lyke Wake Walk of 40 miles (64 km) across the North York Moors; anyone who completes the route within 24 hours can apply for membership of the Lyke Wake Club. Indeed, since the late 1960s, 'Challenge Walking' has become a recognized part of the walking scene with more than 150 events taking place each year. Certificates, cloth badges and even medals are awarded for successful completion of a fixed course. In 1971 the Long Distance Walkers' Association was established with the express purpose of promoting such events and long distance walking generally.

Unfortunately, however, there are some aspects of the walking scene which are far from satisfactory. There are, for example, substantial areas of wild country in England and Wales from which the public is excluded. Despite constant pressure, the old walkers' aim of access over all uncultivated ground is far from being realized. Nor is it true, unfortunately, that all footpaths and bridleways are in a walkable condition. Although farmers are given the privilege, in the interests of efficient husbandry, of ploughing up a footpath which crosses their land (but not a footpath which goes around a field) they are required by law to reinstate it within two weeks. It is a fact that many do not. The result is footpaths that at best are difficult to walk, and at worst are virtually impossible. In any case, there is no doubt that a growing crop on a public path is in practice a real deterrent to most people.

It must also be admitted that in some areas the enormous popularity of walking is producing problems of its own. Some footpaths on the Three Peaks of Yorkshire were so badly affected that a special programme of repair work had to be started in 1987; the summit of Snowdon, which is visited by an incredible number of people each year, was so in need of repair that a similar programme was started in 1977. It must be emphasized, however, that these are exceptional cases requiring exceptional remedies. Nevertheless, it is appropriate to mention that, in one way or another, many features of the countryside which we take for granted are in danger. In guarding our rights, we should also take heed of our responsibilities.

The countryside is there for everybody's enjoyment, whether walker or not; each person finding his or her own pleasure within it. Even so, real appreciation is far more likely to come to the walker than to anyone else—with the possible exception of those who make their living from the land. The walker's quiet approach along footpaths, through woods or down country lanes is generally the more rewarding one, more likely to ferret out secrets, to discover hidden moments. The nest concealed in the corner of a hedgerow, the first bud burst of spring, primrose heads on a grassy bank, the glimpse of a fox, the brilliant blue-green flash of a kingfisher along the line of a stream, the call of an owl breaking the quietness of a gathering dusk. Each belongs to the world, yet each belongs only to the observer. Not one costs anything, yet each is beyond price. All of them are there for the asking along the Walkers' Way.

INTRODUCTION TO THE ROUTE DESCRIPTIONS

1. ACCESS (see page 216)

The routes described later have been walked for a long time without objection and it is not expected that any difficulties will be encountered. Nevertheless, they do in some cases cross country over which there is, strictly speaking, no legal right of way, and in such cases the responsibility must lie with the walker to obtain any necessary permission before crossing such land. In particular, 'short cuts' should not be taken that could cause annoyance to local people. If you encounter any obstruction or difficulty you should contact the appropriate National Park Office (see Council for National Parks in Addresses) for paths within the area.

2. ASCENT

The amount of climbing involved in each route has been estimated from the Outdoor Leisure or Landranger Ordnance Survey maps and should be regarded as approximate only. In some route descriptions specific reference is made to the length and height of individual climbs.

3. CAR-PARKS

Most of the walks start from public car-parks. For other walks parking arrangements are suggested to prevent indiscriminate parking, which can be a great nuisance to local people.

Car break-ins can occur anywhere, even in a National Park. The police advise to take valuables with you or leave them at home; items of value are no longer safe hidden from view in the boot. When parking your vehicle, remember that it is illegal to drive more than 15 yards from the road onto the open moorland.

4. INTERESTING FEATURES ON THE ROUTE

The best position for seeing these is indicated both in the route descriptions and on the maps by *(1)*, *(2)*, etc.

5. LENGTH

These are strictly 'map miles' estimated from the Outdoor Leisure or Landranger maps; no attempt has been made to take into account any ascent or descent involved.

6. MAPS The maps are drawn to a scale of 1:25 000 or 1:50 000 and all names are as given on the Outdoor Leisure or Landranger maps. Field boundaries in particular should be taken as a 'best description'. The maps have been drawn, in the main, so that the route goes from the bottom to the top of a page. The arrow on each map points to grid north. The scale of some small features has been slightly exaggerated for clarity. For easy cross-reference, the relevant Outdoor Leisure and Landranger sheets are indicated on each map.

7. ROUTE DESCRIPTION The letters 'L' and 'R' stand for left and right respectively. Where these are used for changes of direction then they imply a turn of about 90° when facing in the direction of the walk. 'Half L' and 'half R' indicate a half-turn, i.e. approximately 45°, and 'back half L' or 'back half R' indicate three quarter-turns, i.e. about 135°. PFS stands for 'Public Footpath Sign', PBS for 'Public Bridleway Sign' and OS for 'Ordnance Survey'.

To avoid constant repetition, it should be assumed that all stiles and gates mentioned in the route description are to be crossed (unless there is a specific statement otherwise).

8. STANDARD OF THE ROUTES The briefest examination of the route descriptions that follow will show that the routes described cover a wide range of both length and difficulty; some of the easy routes at least can be undertaken by a family party, with care, at most times of the year, while the hardest routes are only really suitable for experienced fellwalkers who are both fit and well-equipped. Any walker therefore who is contemplating following a route should make sure before starting that it is within their ability.

It is difficult in practice, however, to assess the difficulty of any route because it is dependent upon a number of factors and will in any case vary considerably from day to day, even during the day, with the weather. Any consideration of weather conditions must, of course, be left to the walker himself (but read the section on safety and weather first). Apart from that, it is probably best to attempt an overall assessment of difficulty based upon the length, amount of ascent and descent, problems of route-finding and finally, upon the roughness of the terrain. The routes which are not mountainous should never be under-estimated; the going underfoot can be very heavy. Each of the routes has been given a grading based upon a consideration of these factors. A general description of each grade follows:
Easy (1) Generally short walks (up to 6 miles, 9.7 km) over moderately easy ground with no problems of route-finding except in poor visibility. Progress is mostly over fairly gradual

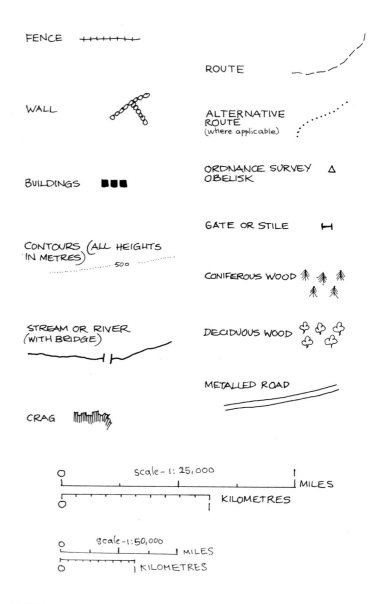

FIGURE 3 *Symbols used on detailed route maps.*

slopes with some short sections of more difficult ground. The paths may, however, sometimes run near steep slopes such as quarry edges; care should be taken here and amongst the moorland clitter.

Moderate (2) Rather longer walks (up to about 10 miles, 16 km) with some routes over paths but where most involve more difficult route-finding across moorland. Tor summits will be reached with climbing over steeper and rougher ground.

More strenuous (3) Longer walks (10–20 miles, 16–32 km) with prolonged spells of climbing. Some rough ground calling for good route-finding ability, particularly in poor weather conditions. The walks are arranged in order of increasing difficulty in each area.

Finally, a summary of each walk is given at the head of each section, with information on the distance, amount of climbing and any special difficulties that will be met along the way.

9. STARTING AND FINISHING POINTS

The majority of the routes are circular in order to avoid any problems with transport when the walk is completed. The location of each starting and finishing point is given by the number of the appropriate Landranger (1:50 000) map with a six-figure grid reference (see page 219); thus (55-854383) indicates a grid reference which can be found on Landranger sheet no. 55.

10. TIME FOR COMPLETION

The usual method of estimating the length of time needed for a walk is by Naismith's Rule: 'For ordinary walking allow one hour for every 3 miles (5 km) and add one hour for every 2000 feet (600 m) of ascent; for backpacking with a heavy load allow one hour for every 2½ miles (4 km) and one hour for every 1500 feet (450 m) of ascent.' However, for many this tends to be over-optimistic and it is better for each walker to form an assessment of his or her own performance over one or two walks. Naismith's Rule also makes no allowance for rest or food stops or for the influence of weather conditions.

TO MALHAM COVE

STARTING AND FINISHING
POINT
Malham National Park Centre
car-park (98-900627)
LENGTH
2 miles (3 km)
ASCENT
200 feet (60 m)

The Cove, a magnificent and overhanging precipice 240 feet (73 m) high is one of the most impressive sights in the Yorkshire Dales. It provided the inspiration for Charles Kingsley's *The Water Babies* and in more recent years has been the scene of some of the most difficult and exposed climbs on British limestone. The route from Malham to the Cove along the west side of Malham Beck is very popular, the return over pastures to the east is quieter and better.

ROUTE DESCRIPTION (Map 1)

Leave the large car-park in Malham *(1)* turning L down the minor road past the Information Centre. At the road turn L again and walk to the stone bridge at the centre of the village. Do not cross the bridge, but continue on the road ahead (signpost to Malham Tarn, Langcliffe and Settle). A few yards along, after the telephone box, turn R and then immediately L through a small gate (PFS 'Pennine Way'); this leads to a short

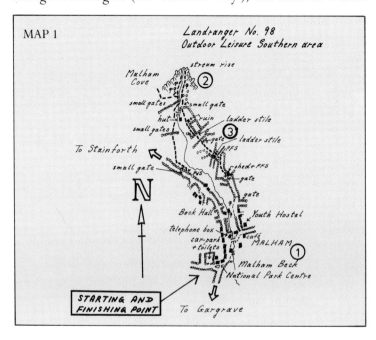

Near Malham Cove. The walk returns to Malham along the opposite side of the stream.

but delightful path by the river which is a much better alternative to the road itself. Further along rejoin the road and continue in the same direction. After about 500 yards (460 m) from the bridge in Malham, pass a farmhouse on your R; here the road begins to climb steeply (road sign '1:7 single track road with passing places'). Follow the road up the hill; 175 yards (160 m) after a barn on the R go through a small gate in the wall to the R (Pennine Way sign).

The great cliff of Malham Cove can now be seen directly ahead. Follow the very clear path which heads directly for the Cove. The path crosses a wall at a small gate and then heads slightly R to the bank of the stream. Pass a footbridge, cross a second wall and continue along the bank to reach the cliff at its centre where the stream emerges *(2)*. There are very few places within the Yorkshire Dales — or indeed anywhere, for that matter — more impressive than this spot at the foot of the Cove.

You can return from here by the same route, but it is much better instead to use a footpath on the opposite side of the stream. Cross the stream and walk down on the other bank to a small gate (PFS 'Malham $\frac{3}{4}$'). (When there is too much water to make the crossing, use the footbridge lower down.) At the small gate do not go to the footbridge, but instead go on a path slightly L, soon climbing up a bank (yellow waymarks). At the top continue in the same direction with the steep slope of the bank to your R. Pass to the R of a ruined barn and then follow a wall to a ladder stile in a corner *(3)*. Cross the next field to a gate. Continue in the same direction to a PFS 'Malham/The Cove') and then to the L of a ruined (but substantial) wall, to a further ladder stile. Go between walls (PFS) and then half R across a narrow field to a gate by a small shed in the far L-hand corner (PFS 'Malham/The Cove'). Enter a walled lane and follow it back to Malham, reaching the village by the Youth Hostel.

1 Malham

The exact derivation of the name Malham is not clear, but it may mean 'stony or gravelly place', a name which would be in keeping with much of its surrounding area. In the Domesday Book the name is given as 'Malgun' whilst thirteenth century records show it as 'Malghum' or 'Malgum'. In any event there has been a settlement at Malham for well over one thousand years and human habitation in the area for perhaps three thousand. Today it is without doubt the most popular village in the National Park with one million visitors each year; partly because it is within easy reach of the large industrial towns to the south and east and partly because it is near to three of the most impressive features of the Dales, the Cove, the Tarn and Gordale Scar.

The present bridge which marks the centre of the village is eighteenth century but incorporates much of an earlier pack-horse bridge of the seventeenth, while there are three clapper bridges of earlier origin. The Buck Inn is comparatively recent, but Lister's Arms bears the date 1723. Beck Hall by the road to the Cove is Tudor. The Youth Hostel is one of a chain of hostels along the Pennine Way and, with Ingleton Hostel, the largest in the Park.

2 Malham Cove

The Middle Craven Fault, running roughly east to west just north of Malham, marks the southern limit of the Great Scar Limestone, for the land to the south of it is of a very different character. The Cove and the valley in front of it were created when glacial melt waters ran down the steep hillside produced by the fault and eroded back cutting into the edge of the limestone bed. It is a magnificent sight: a great natural amphitheatre with sheer — and, in parts, overhanging —

Malham Cove

walls tapering back into the hillsides on each side. The stream of icy water issuing from its foot sank underground at Smelt Mill Sink about $1\frac{1}{2}$ miles (2.5 km) to the north-west. As at Gordale Scar house martins build their nests each year under the great overhangs and the birds are a familiar sight in June wheeling and swooping over the huge face.

Magnificent as it may still be, the Cove has, in fact, lost a little of its glory over the years, for the depression in the centre of the cliff was originally the lip of a waterfall, about three times higher than any existing fall in the Dales today. Not since the early years of the nineteenth century however has any water been known to flow over it.

To the rock climber the Cove is the finest crag in the Dales, with about one hundred routes up to 600 feet (180 m) in length. The huge and very impressive Central Wall, directly above the stream exit, was first climbed in 1959.

3 *Iron-Age field boundaries*
The first two fields after leaving the road on the walk to Malham Cove are crossed by a series of parallel ridges running down the hillside towards the stream. These are the remains of Iron-Age field boundaries probably worked about the third century AD. Similar remains can be found at other sites in the Dales.

1.2

Cautley Spout

STARTING AND FINISHING
POINT
Cross Keys Temperance Hotel, $4\frac{1}{2}$
miles (7.5 km) from Sedbergh on the
A683 to Kirkby Stephen (98-698969).
A few cars may be parked in the small
lay-by above the footbridge at the
start of the walk
LENGTH
$2\frac{1}{2}$ miles (4 km)
ASCENT
500 feet (150 m)

Cautley Spout, on the eastern flank of the Howgills overlooking
the Rawthey valley, is one of the most spectacular waterfalls in
the National Park. A magnificent cascade of white water
hundreds of feet long, its visual impact is heightened considerably by its position at the centre of a huge valley of rock and
scree. It is easily and quickly reached from the Cross Keys Hotel
on the Sedbergh–Kirkby Stephen road by a pleasant path which
follows the north bank of Cautley Holme Beck. The only
climbing (which can be omitted) takes place towards the end
where the path rises to a viewpoint above the Spout.

Route Description (Map 2)

Descend to the footbridge and cross to the opposite bank of the

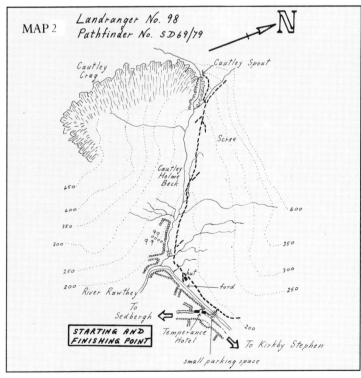

MAP 2   Landranger No. 98 Pathfinder No. SD69/79

N

Cautley Crag

Cautley Spout

Scree

Cautley Holme Beck

450

400

350

200

250

200

River Rawthey

400

350

300

250

hut

ford

200

To Sedbergh

Temperance Hotel

To Kirkby Stephen

small parking space

STARTING AND FINISHING POINT

The Cross Keys Temperance Hotel. The walk goes up the valley behind the hotel.

stream. There turn L and follow a path going downstream on the R bank. Pass a small hut and soon afterwards at a stream junction turn R. Follow the path to the R of the subsidiary stream (the Spout is now obvious on the hillside ahead) crossing a large mound in the base of the valley and finally rising to a good viewpoint at the top of the main fall. Return by the same route. Care should be taken on the final rise by the Spout where the drop to the stream is considerable.

Cautley Crag and the Spout under winter snow

1.3

GORDALE SCAR AND MALHAM COVE

STARTING AND FINISHING
POINT
Malham National Park Centre
car-park (98-900627)
LENGTH
4¾ miles (7.5 km)
ASCENT
650 feet (200 m)

Gordale Scar, a magnificent ravine with overhanging walls 150 feet (45 m) high, is rivalled only by Malham Cove as the most impressive sight in the Yorkshire Dales. This route includes both. Waymarks have been placed throughout. A short and easy but superb walk in magnificent limestone country. Janet's Foss and Little Gordale, also on the route, would be worth a visit on their own account, but on this route are dwarfed in comparison with the Cove and Scar.

ROUTE DESCRIPTION (Map 3)

Leave the car-park in Malham *(1)* and turn L down a minor road

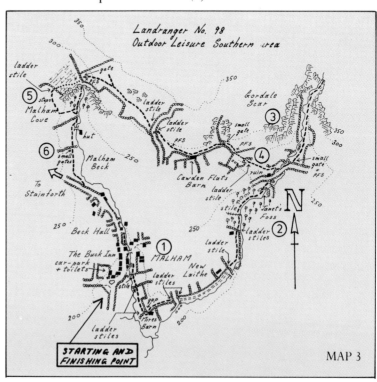

Opposite *Gordale Scar*

past the Information Centre. At the road turn L again. Opposite Sparth House, which is just before the Buck Inn, turn R and cross the stream over a small footbridge. On the far side turn R and walk downstream. Soon, cross a stile and then follow the path across two fields to reach a ladder stile in a wall corner. Immediately after the ladder stile bend L with the wall and go through a gap just before a barn. Follow the wall (which is now on your R), soon crossing a ladder stile into a lane.

Go ahead for 25 yards (23 m) to a further ladder stile. Cross and follow the clear path by a wall to reach still another ladder stile just past a barn. Beyond, follow the path to the L of a stream, then follow a wall to twin ladder stiles, and finally continue on through a beautiful ravine (Little Gordale) to reach a waterfall, Janet's Foss *(2)*. The path goes up to the L to a road.

Turn R along the road. Immediately after a bridge and bend in the road go L through a small gate. The way ahead is now obvious, along a very clear path as far as the lower waterfall within the great ravine of Gordale Scar *(3)*. Do not attempt to go further up the ravine, but instead retrace your route back to the road and turn R. After the bend go R over the old bridge and immediately R again over a ladder stile.

Go half L to a wall corner and climb the hill ahead keeping by the wall. At the top *(4)* cross a ladder stile and go half R to a second ladder stile. Here, turn L on a grassy path keeping the wall on your L. Pass through a small gate (notice the dry valley to the R) and keep in the same direction with the wall. After a barn where the wall bends L leave the wall to continue in the same direction across open ground to reach a road.

Cross the road, go over the ladder stile opposite and along a path half R which leaves the walls to L and R. Eventually you will reach the wall again on your L at a corner where the path forks. Take the L fork which descends to a gate in a wall. The edge of the Malham Cove precipice *(5)* will now be obvious a short distance to your L. (This edge is not fenced and should be approached with great care.)

Cross the limestone pavements keeping well to the R of the cliff edge to reach a ladder stile on the far side. Cross and descend L on a clear path. Lower down below the cliff turn L with the path heading directly towards the stream. Near to the stream the path bends to the R. (It is worthwhile making a short detour here to the L to the foot of the Cove where the stream emerges.) Follow the path keeping to the R side of the stream to eventually reach a road *(6)*. Turn L and follow the road back to Malham. Or better still, go L over the stile from the road immediately after Beck Hall and follow a secluded footpath on the R bank of the stream back to the centre of the village.

1 Malham   See page 18.

2 Janet's Foss

The small but delightful waterfall of Janet's Foss, and the wooded limestone gorge of 'Little Gordale', make a fitting introduction to the much greater glories of the Scar itself. 'Foss' is an old Norse word for waterfall whilst Janet was reputedly the queen of the local fairies who lived in the cave behind the fall. The original rock face responsible for the waterfall now lies behind a screen of tufa, a soft porous limestone, built over it by the stream. A good time to visit the Foss is mid-May when the floor of the ravine is covered with a carpet of wild garlic.

3 Gordale Scar

Arguably the two most spectacular sights in the Yorkshire Dales lie near to each other within one mile of Malham village — Malham Cove and Gordale Scar — both formed in a similar manner by stream erosion back into the scarp of the Middle Craven Fault. But there the similarity ends. The glories of the Cove are an obvious feature before you as you approach along Malham Beck. The glories of Gordale by contrast are hidden away, to be revealed only at the last moment when the walker turns the corner into the extremity of the gorge. The huge overhanging walls of Great Scar Limestone, the deep shadow, the chill and the menace of the great ravine of Gordale impress all who go there.

It is likely that the ravine is a collapsed cave system, the stream originally disappearing down a swallow hole on the moor beyond. The rock step by the lower fall was also extensively covered with tufa, although this is now being rapidly worn away.

Some very hard rock-climbing has been seen upon the walls of Gordale. The first major route completed was the West Face Route in 1954 by D. Farley and N. Rhodes; this is a very severe route of 220 feet (70 m) which goes up the right wall of the ravine just above the lower waterfall. There are now about 130 routes on the Scar covering all the main faces.

4 Lynchets

An obvious feature of the Malham area, particularly to the east and west of Malham Beck, are the series of giant terraces or steps, each 100–200 yards (90–180 m) long, cut into and across the hillsides. They are called lynchets, a feature to be found both in other parts of the Dales and outside it in areas such as Cambridgeshire and Dorset. The ones in the Malham area were cut by Anglian farmers in the eighth century to produce the extra food needed by the growing villages, when the more suitable land in the valleys had been fully exploited.

The terraces, made by clearing and then levelling the ground, were essential for the teams of oxen used in ploughing which otherwise were unmanageable on steep hill slopes.

5 *Malham Cove*   See page 20.
6 *Iron-age field boundaries*   See page 22.

Malham Cove

BOLTON ABBEY AND THE STRID

STARTING AND FINISHING
POINT
Bolton Abbey car-park (104-071539)
LENGTH
6½ miles (10.5 km)
ASCENT
100 feet (30 m)

Bolton Abbey and Bolton Woods are extremely popular in the summer months. The best time for this walk therefore is out-of-season when the crowds are elsewhere. The ruins and chapel of Bolton Abbey, beautiful woods and the impressive Strid are the main attractions along a particularly lovely stretch of the Wharfe. A straightforward walk, with virtually no climbing, which barely makes the moderate category. Bolton Woods is a conservation area, so please keep to the footpaths. A small fee should be paid on leaving the woods by the Cavendish Pavilion on the return route.

ROUTE DESCRIPTION (Map 4)

Leave the car-park to the R of the toilet block and village hall and walk along the minor road to a junction. Cross the road half L and go through the small gate in the gap in the high wall on the opposite side (sign 'To the Priory'). Follow the path beyond down to a footbridge over the river. On the far bank turn L and after a few yards go R up some steps at a path junction. Follow the path for ⅔ mile (1.1 km) to a road.

Go L along the road, soon crossing a ford over a footbridge. Immediately after the ford take the path on the L going R over a stile to follow a path on the R bank of the river. Cross a minor road by a bridge (refreshments are available at the Cavendish Pavilion on the opposite bank) and continue along the path on the R bank of the stream, soon reaching a road. Go L along the road, over a small bridge and then leave it to the L again after a few yards to continue in the same direction along a footpath. Follow this footpath alongside the river to reach the Strid (1). Care should be taken on this section as some scrambling is required. Beyond, continue on the R bank, rising R to a stile after ½ mile (800 m). Follow the path to an aqueduct (2) over the river, and cross this to the opposite bank.

Turn L along the path by the river and walk downstream,

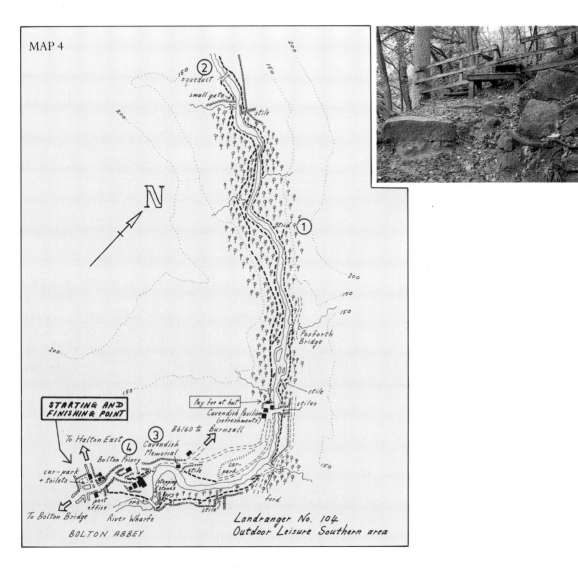

MAP 4

To Halton East

STARTING AND FINISHING POINT

car-park + toilets

Bolton Priory

post office

To Bolton Bridge

River Wharfe

BOLTON ABBEY

Cavendish Memorial

stepping stones

B6160 to Burnsall

Cavendish Pavilion (refreshments)

Pay fee at hut

car-park

stile

stiles

ford

stile

Posforth Bridge

Strid

stile

small gate

aqueduct

Landranger No. 104
Outdoor Leisure Southern area

soon re-entering the woods at a small gate. Follow the clear path through the woods above the river to reach the Cavendish Pavilion again after 1½ miles (2.5 km); there is a choice of routes along this section, either low down by the river or higher up the hillside. As the woods are private property and contain a number of nature trails, in spring and summer a small entrance fee must be paid at the small hut on leaving the woods.

Continue past the Pavilion and by the river to the far end of the large parking/picnic area. At the end, take a path which goes half R across open ground rising at the end to a stile and road. Turn L along the road past a fountain (3) — there are lovely views down to the L over the river and the Priory. After 300 yards (275 m) where the road bends R go L through a small gate. Pass to the R of the Priory church (4) and then along the drive curving R to the road. Turn L for the car-park.

1 The Strid

At the Strid, the Wharfe, which shortly before was up to 60 feet (18 m) wide, is forced through a narrow rock ravine barely 6–8 feet ($2-2\frac{1}{2}$ m). The result is a mad frenzy of white water rushing and sliding its way through the gap into sinister black pools below. The rocks on each side are smoothed and rounded by the action of the water, and just near enough to tempt. Attempts to jump the Strid have however cost a few people their lives.

2 The Aqueduct

The aqueduct crossing the Wharfe just south of Barden Bridge carries water from the reservoirs in Nidderdale to Bradford.

3 The Cavendish Memorial Fountain

The tall structure on the roadside at the top of the entrance to the Cavendish Pavilion car-park is a covered fountain erected by the electors of the West Riding as a tribute to the memory of Frederick Charles Cavendish (born 30 November, 1836. Died 6 May, 1882.) A further memorial in the form of a cross, erected by the tenantry of the Bolton Abbey estates, is in the churchyard.

Frederick Charles Cavendish, son of the 7th Duke of Devonshire, was appointed Chief Secretary for Ireland by Gladstone in 1882. On 6 May, only a few hours after his arrival in Ireland, he was stabbed to death with his undersecretary T. H. Burke while walking in Phoenix Park, Dublin. The assassins were a group of Irish extremists known as the Invincibles. It appears that Burke was the actual target, Cavendish being killed while trying to defend him against his attackers. The murder effectively stopped any attempts to solve the Irish problem for several years.

4 Bolton Priory

In 1120 a Priory of Augustinian Canons (Black Canons) was founded at Embsay about 4 miles (6.5 km) to the west of Bolton Abbey. This was moved in 1151 to the present — and much more attractive — site by Alicia de Romilly whose parents had established the original Priory at Embsay. The church and some domestic buildings for the Canons were built in the twelfth century, with further building in the fourteenth, considerably extending the size of the Priory. Work on the West Tower was begun in 1520 but never completed, the Dissolution reaching the Priory in 1539. The Nave of the church was spared and is now used as the Priory

Bolton Priory

Bolton Woods

Church of Bolton Abbey, with the chancel and transepts forming impressive ruins behind. Recently, a national appeal exceeded expectations by raising £400,000 for essential repair and restoration work on this church which attracts some 200,000 visitors from all corners of the earth each year. The work included the roofing of the West Tower.

The beautiful hall facing the west doorway of the church is Bolton Hall, a private residence of the Duke of Devonshire. The square centre tower is the old gateway of the Priory which was left intact at the Dissolution. The south wing was added in 1720 and the north wing in 1843.

The Old Rectory to the south of the Priory ruins was built in 1700 as the result of a bequest by Robert Boyle to his nephew, Charles, Earl of Burlington, of a sum of money to be used for charitable purposes. The building was used as a school and as a house for the headmaster until 1874, when it became the rectory which it remained until 1978. An inscribed (in Latin) stone on the building describes the bequest. Robert Boyle is much better known for his scientific achievements and in particular for 'Boyle's Law' which was named after him.

2.5

THE ASCENT OF WHERNSIDE

STARTING AND FINISHING
POINT
Ribblehead (98-765793) at the
junction of B6255 and B6479
between Ingleton and Hawes
LENGTH
7½ miles (12 km)
ASCENT
1500 feet (460 m)

As the highest mountain in Yorkshire, Whernside inevitably attracts the crowds, although, in my opinion, both Ingleborough and Pen-y-ghent are superior. The old route up the mountain left from directly between Ivescar and Winterscales. This was always long and tedious, and with the passage of time it had also grown muddy — very muddy. An example of the damage that can be caused by thousands of heavy boots — and many not nearly so heavy — tramping up and down, day in and day out, throughout the year. For that reason, and in order to allow the ghastly scar on the face to grass over, an alternative route (which is in any case immeasurably superior and will therefore give a lot more pleasure) has been arranged by the National Park Authority. It is the route described here — a 'must' for railway enthusiasts.

ROUTE DESCRIPTION (Maps 5–7)

From the T-junction walk towards the railway bridge, turning R along the farm road just before the Station Inn. Continue past the viaduct (1) to a wall at the far end. Follow a path to the R of the railway to the Blea Moor signal box. After the box continue along the clear path to the R of the railway (and later with a stream) to an aqueduct over the railway line. Cross the aqueduct and follow the path beyond on the R side of the stream.

The large waterfall further along is Force Gill. From the vicinity of the Gill take a path which goes away to the R to the R of a fence. Follow this, later crossing the fence at a stile. Follow a path on the opposite side which curves half R across the moor. This later curves to the L and rises up to the summit ridge of Whernside. Turn L to the summit (OS obelisk).

Continue beyond the summit with the wall to your R. After about ¾ mile (1.2 km) descend over two small patches of scree; at the bottom of the second patch by a large cairn go half L and descend steeply to a ladder stile. Continue descending to a

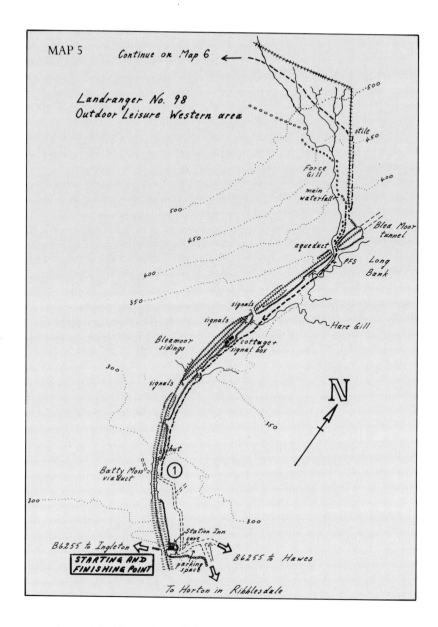

MAP 5   *Continue on Map 6* ←

*Landranger No. 98
Outdoor Leisure Western area*

Force Gill

main waterfall

aqueduct

Blea Moor tunnel

PFS   Long Bank

stile

Hare Gill

signals

signals

Bleamoor sidings

cottage signal box

signals

hut

Batty Moss viaduct

①

N

Station Inn cave

B6255 to Ingleton

STARTING AND FINISHING POINT

parking space

B6255 to Hawes

To Horton in Ribblesdale

---

second ladder stile and then across a field to a third ladder stile in the far R-hand corner. Immediately after the stile go L through a small gate (i.e. to the R of a barn).

Head towards a farmhouse, passing through a gate and then to the R of barns to a small gate. Continue in the same general direction over four fields (there is a scar and a waterfall to the L) to Ivescar. Go between barns and the house, turning R before the final large barn. Turn L through a gate immediately after the barn and cross the field half R to a gate on the far side. In the next field follow the L-hand wall (crossing a fence) to a stile in the wall corner. Cross the next field half R to a further gate and then cross the final field to a gate which leads into a road. Turn

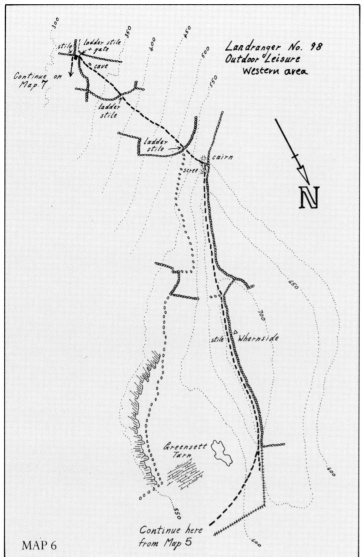

Landranger No. 98
Outdoor Leisure
Western area

MAP 6

L. After a gate across the road, turn R over a bridge and follow the farm road back to Ribblehead.

1 The Settle–Carlisle railway

The construction of the Settle–Carlisle railway by the Midland Railway Company, in the six years between 1869 and 1875, was a major achievement in civil engineering. The aim of the project was to give the Midlands a main trunk route from London to Scotland via Bedford and Derby, which would enable it to compete with its main rivals, the Great Northern Railway which operated the East Coast Route through York and the London and North Western Railway operating a West Coast Route through Crewe.

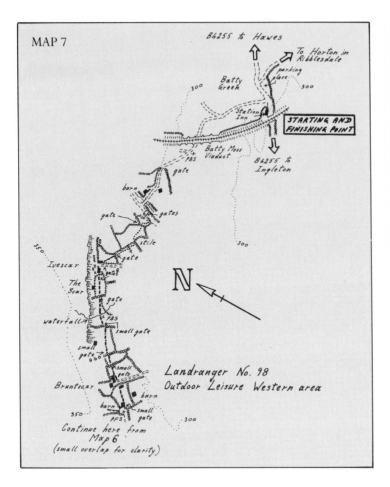

MAP 7

B6255 to Hawes

To Horton in
Ribblesdale

parking
place

Batty
Green

300

300

Station
Inn

STARTING AND
FINISHING POINT

Batty Moss
Viaduct

B6255 to
Ingleton

PBS

gate

barn

gate

gates

300

stile

550

gate

N

Ivescar

gate

The
Scar

gate

waterfall

PBS

small gate

small
gate

small
gate

Bruntscar

barn

barn

350

PFS

small
gate

300

Landranger No. 98
Outdoor Leisure Western area

Continue here from
Map 6
(small overlap for clarity)

From the outset it was clear that the forcing of a line
through an area of high fell and deep valleys would be a
formidable one. Railway lines have to be relatively level, with
a rise or fall of only a few feet in a mile, and fairly straight. It
was these requirements which necessitated the profusion of
viaducts, cuttings, embankments and tunnels which are
characteristic of the Settle–Carlisle.

In the 72 miles (116 km) of track between Settle and
Carlisle there are no less than twelve tunnels and fifteen
viaducts. The Ribblehead Viaduct (originally Batty Moss
Viaduct and so called on the Outdoor Leisure Map) has
twenty-four arches, is a quarter of a mile long (400 m) and
rises about 100 feet (30 m) above the ground; there are also
six others with lengths of about 200 yards (180 m). The
longest tunnel, the Blea Moor, is 2,629 yards (2.4 km) long
with a depth of about 500 feet (150 m) at its deepest point.

Whernside from Greensett Tarn

The Ribblehead Viaduct

The construction of the line required a vast army of workers who were brought in from all over the country and housed in shanty towns along the line of work. Maiming and death from disease or accident were unfortunate, but common, features of everyday life. In the south porch of the Parish Church at Settle and on the west wall of the small church at Chapel le Dale are memorial tablets to those who lost their lives.

The two most impressive features of the line can be seen from Route 5, the Ribblehead Viaduct and the entrance to the Blea Moor Tunnel. On the moor slope behind the tunnel entrance are the shafts used in construction, and since for ventilation, with adjacent spoil heaps of excavated material.

ARKENGARTHDALE

STARTING AND FINISHING
POINT
Reeth (98-039993)
LENGTH
11½ miles (18 km)
ASCENT
1600 feet (490 m)

Arkengarthdale is the most northerly of the National Park dales, running from Reeth to the north-west between the summit of Calver Hill and the imposing line of Fremington Edge. This route runs in a clockwise direction around Calver Hill over Reeth Low Moor, crossing the Dale at Langthwaite, and returning along Fremington Edge. The moorland tracks of short springy turf over Reeth Low Moor are superb, as are the views later in the walk from Fremington Edge, but followers of the television series *All Creatures Great and Small* will be more impressed perhaps by the old bridge in Langthwaite which was featured in the programme.

ROUTE DESCRIPTION (Maps 8–10)

From the green at the centre of Reeth turn up Silver Street (B6270) by the Buck Hotel. Walk past the fire station and beyond the houses for 350 yards (320 m), then turn R up a narrow path between walls (PFS 'Skellgate'). Follow this delightful lane through L and R bends to its end at a gate. Continue ahead along a clear path with a wall to the L, contouring the hillside.

After ¾ mile (1.2 km) where the wall bends L, continue ahead to a junction where go L, dropping down by a house (Moorcock House) to a lower farm road. Turn R, soon passing a farm on your L. 200 yards (180 m) after the farm go R at a junction. Soon pass a wall on your L and shortly afterwards go R at a further junction for a few yards to another wall. Continue with this wall on your R. Where the wall bends round to the R, continue in the same direction (no path) soon picking up a path which climbs the ridge ahead. Continue over the ridge on the path which soon becomes much clearer. Follow the path across the moor to a gate by a road (the famous 'water-splash' featured in the television series *All Creatures Great and Small* is just down to the left).

Do not go through the gate, but turn back half R along a very obvious track. Follow this magnificent moorland track of short

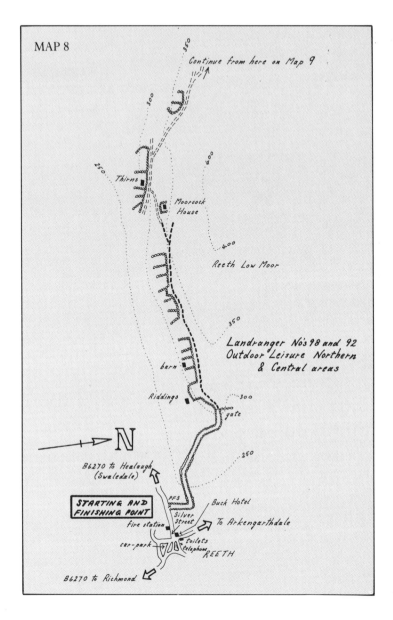

MAP 8

Continue from here on Map 9

Thirns

Moorcock House

Reeth Low Moor

Landranger No's 98 and 92
Outdoor Leisure Northern
& Central areas

barn

Riddings

gate

N

B6270 to Healaugh
(Swaledale)

STARTING AND
FINISHING POINT

PFS

Buck Hotel

Silver
Street

fire station

To Arkengarthdale

car-park

toilets
telephone

REETH

B6270 to Richmond

springy turf between massed banks of heather for 1¼ miles
(2 km), gradually descending to the road in Arkengarthdale
(1) — there is just one path junction on the way, at this keep L.
Turn L along the road and follow it to the village of
Langthwaite.

In the village turn R over the bridge and immediately R again
on to the river side. Follow the path downstream on the L bank
of the river. After ½ mile (800 m) the path leaves the river to the
L through a wood; at a PFS at the far end of the wood go L (i.e.

Reeth

46

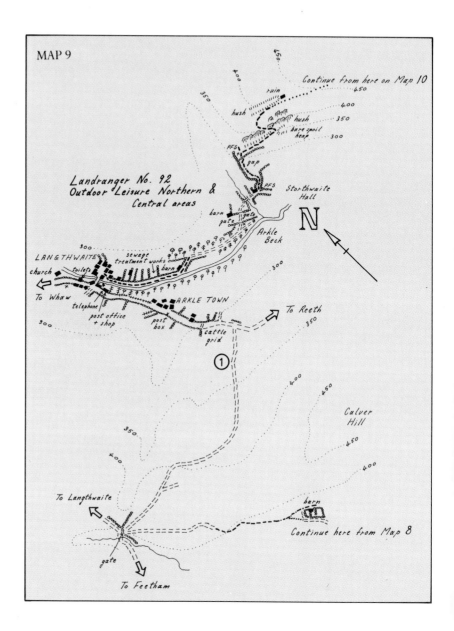

MAP 9

Continue from here on Map 10

450
400
350
300

400
350

ruin
hush
hush
bare spoil
heap

Landranger No. 92
Outdoor Leisure Northern &
Central areas

PFS
gap

PFS
Storthwaite
Hall

barn
gate

gate

N

300

LANGTHWAITE
sewage
treatment works
barn

Arkle
Beck

church
toilets

To Whaw
telephone
post office
+ shop

ARKLE TOWN

post
box

To Reeth
350

cattle
grid

①

300

400
450

Calver
Hill
450

350
400

400

To Langthwaite

barn

Continue here from Map 8

gate

To Feetham

to Fremington). Follow the farm road to a footbridge by a ford,
cross and go to the farmhouse ahead. Immediately after the first
house turn L up a lane (PFS 'Hurst'). Where the lane ends
continue up the field with a wall on your L to a wall gap at the
top of the field. Turn R (PFS) and go up to the R of a hush (a
ravine produced by lead miners).

After 400 yards (370 km), at the foot of a large bare spoil
heap, turn back half L climbing up a grassy path. The path soon
bends R and goes to the R of a second hush. Where this hush
ends, continue in the same direction over the moor by some
spoil heaps (no path) to reach a gate at a wall corner. Go
through the gate and continue in the same direction along

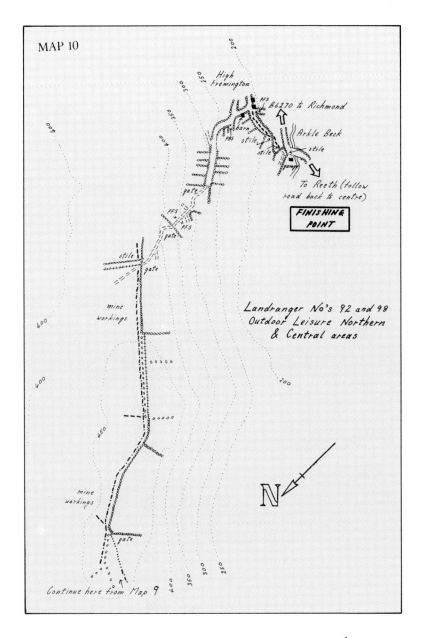

MAP 10

High Fremington

B6270 to Richmond

Arkle Beck

stile

To Reeth (follow road back to centre)

FINISHING POINT

Landranger No's 92 and 98
Outdoor Leisure Northern
& Central areas

stile

gate

mine workings

mine workings

gate

N

Continue here from Map 9

Fremington Edge with a wall to your R. Continue for 1¼ miles (2 km) to a stile in a crossing fence.

Do not cross the stile, but instead go through a gate on the R. Descend the hillside on a clear path, later reaching a road. Lower down the road descends through a wood and immediately afterwards bends L with a bridleway (PBS 'Arkengarthdale') coming in on the R. Continue along the road for 55 yards (50 m) more then, where the road bends L, turn R down a narrow path. At the bottom turn R on the road and then almost immediately leave it again to the R at a gate and stile. The path beyond follows the wall soon passing through a stile. Further along cross over another stile on the L and then over two meadows to reach a road near to a bridge. Go R over the bridge back to Reeth.

1 Arkengarthdale

As with those of upper Swaledale the place-names of Arkengarthdale show signs of Norse settlement. Arkengarthdale itself is 'the valley of Arnkell's (or Arkil's) enclosure', Arnkell being a common Old Scandinavian name, whilst Langthwaite was 'a long clearing'. At the mouth of the Dale the influence is Anglian, however, as shown by the 'tun' villages, such as Grinton and Fremington.

The Dale was an important centre for lead mining, particularly from the beginning of the seventeenth century, the miners living in local villages, such as Langthwaite, Whaw and Arkle Town. Several hushes can be seen on both sides of Slei Gill and there were smelt mills both there and further up the Dale near Langthwaite. Considerable depopulation of the Dale took place in the nineteenth century due to the decline of the industry, with mining families moving southwards to the Lancashire cotton towns and eastwards into Durham.

1.7

Ancient and Modern Trackways

STARTING AND FINISHING
POINT
Grosmont car-park (94-825053) to
the west of the A169 Whitby to
Pickering road at Sleights.
LENGTH
4¼ miles (7.5 km)
ASCENT
400 feet (120 m)

The first half of the walk follows part of the route of the Whitby–Pickering railway, which was opened in 1836. There is an opportunity to view the workshops of the North York Moors Railway and the engines awaiting restoration. The walk continues through the wooded valley of the Murk Esk to the picturesque hamlet of Beck Hole. The return to Grosmont involves a climb onto the edge of the moors and later a walk beside an ancient paved pannierway through Crag Cliff Wood.

Route Description (Map 11)

From the car-park turn L to the level crossing at Grosmont Station *(1)*. Turn R after the crossing through a gate signposted 'Footpath to Goathland'. Cross over a footbridge and bear L up a track which passes the church. On your R are the railway and footpath tunnels which give access to the North York Moors Railway engine sheds; the small tunnel was used by the original horse-drawn railway. Turn half R through a gate, continuing to climb, and after 50 yards (45 m) turn L through a gate (PFS). Follow the distinct track downhill keeping a wire fence on your L. Before reaching the railway line you pass a viewing area overlooking the railway's workshops *(2)*.

Pass through a gate down to the lineside and continue to a small gate which gives access to a broad track beside the line. Engines awaiting restoration are usually parked on this section of line. Continue along the side of the railway until the broad track *(3)* leaves the railway and leads into the hamlet of Esk Valley *(4)*. The track runs straight on through the wooded valley of the Murk Esk to a footbridge which crosses the river, using the original bridge pillars for support. Continuing along the track you eventually reach a few steps by the river bank, pass through the wood to a stile, and a track then leads straight on into the picturesque hamlet of Beck Hole *(5)*.

Turn L and follow the road steeply uphill. At the sharp bend

51

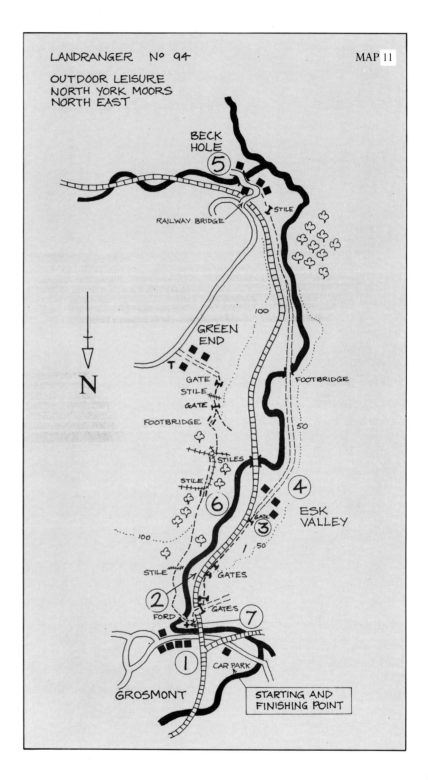

there is an elevated view over the hamlet. Cross over the railway
bridge and at a junction turn L along the road for ¼ mile (1.2
km) to Green End. At the telephone box turn L down through

Cottage at Beck Hole

the hamlet; at the end of the road turn R through a flagged gateway (PBS) and in 20 yards (18 m) bear L over a stile along a flagged path between walls, then continue straight on between hedges with the flagged path on the R of the farm track. Pass through a gate and immediately bear half R (PFS). The path descends to a bridge and then through open woodland. After crossing a stile into a wood, turn R to another stile into a field and turn L along the edge of the wood to a stile and footbridge into Crag Cliff Wood.

Continue along the path where you begin to see the best section of the ancient paved way *(6)*. Follow the path as people have done for centuries, pass out of the wood over a stile, and the paved way continues down the field to join a road. Turn L through a gate which crosses the road, turn L again just before the ford and walk over a large footbridge. Climb the steps to the path which leads to a lane. Turn L up the lane and then R through the stile at the church *(7)*. Continue through the churchyard and pass over a stile into the lane you departed on earlier. Turn R over the footbridge into Grosmont.

1 *Grosmont*

The village owes its existence to the discovery of ironstone when the railway was constructed. There were eight ironstone mines in the area and the car-park was the site of three blast furnaces which finally closed in 1915. Time and nature have mellowed all these sites.

2 *North York Moors Railway*

The Whitby–Pickering railway line was opened in 1836. The line was surveyed and constructed by George Stephenson, who designed the *Rocket*. Originally the coaches were pulled by horses and were shaped like a stage-coach—they carried six passengers inside, four outside in front, four behind and as many as could get on top! One horse was required to pull each carriage, with two required on the hills. On downhill sections, as from Beck Hole to Grosmont, the horses rode in dandy carts coupled to the coaches. At Goathland the carriages were drawn up an incline and reassembled to continue the journey. The line was converted to steam in 1847 and a deviation line, around the incline, was built along the present route in 1865. Under the 'Beeching Plan' the line south of Grosmont closed in 1965. The historic and scenic value of the line was recognized and a preservation society was formed. Since then volunteers and a few full-time officials have turned the line into a tourist attraction carrying over 200,000 passengers annually on both steam- and diesel-hauled trains.

3 *The original railway line*

Your path into Esk Valley was the original line constructed by George Stephenson. One of the sources of revenue for the line in the first few decades was stone and later iron ore; as you walk down the broad path you can see the brick-faced shaft-top of the Esk Valley Ironstone Mine on your right in a field. The mine opened in 1859 and closed some time after 1862. When it reopened in 1871 the extra shaft had to be built as a result of new laws following the New Hartley Colliery Disaster in Northumberland, when the only way into the mine was sealed as the pithead gear collapsed trapping 204 mineworkers.

4 *Esk Valley*

The hamlet of Esk Valley was built for workers at the nearby ironstone and whinstone mines. The first large building on the right had two upstairs floors as living quarters for four families of craftsmen at the iron mine, which was 60 yards

Steaming up, Grosmont

(55 m) away on the hillside. The ground floor at the back of the building served as workshops and the mine office. The railway was the only connection with the outside world; every two weeks a train brought coal and other goods to the hamlet. When the track became unusable in 1951, the residents raised the money to construct a road to join the Goathland to Lease Rigg road.

5 *Beck Hole*

The hamlet of stone houses nestles in a hollow under the moors formed by Ellerbeck. West Beck and Ellerbeck join close to Beck Hole and form the Murk Esk. There is a fine view of the hamlet from the foot of the road to Goathland, past the inn and the bridge to the green. On summer evenings the game of quoits is played on the green as part of a local league. The players throw a metal ring weighing 5¼ pounds (2.4 kg) across an 11 yard (10 m) pitch. The idea is to throw the quoit over a metal pin—a ringer—or set the quoit against the pin to prevent your opponent getting a ringer—a gater. The pins are surrounded by a soft area in which the quoits will stick when they land. The ones on Beck Hole green are protected by square boxes.

6 *Paved ways*

The paved ways were used by pannier ponies as the stones were wide enough for ponies but not for wheeled vehicles. The paved sections were usually on the steeper slopes, where traffic would erode the surface, but a few of them ran for miles across the moors. The ponies carried their loads in panniers balanced on either side of their backs. A train of twenty to forty ponies were usually headed by a lead pony wearing bells. Moorland coal was moved by this method around Rosedale as late as the 1870s.

7 *Grosmont Church*

The original church building was opened on 1 June 1842 to meet the needs of the expanding community, and by 1875 the present larger church had to be built. To help raise funds for the original church a three day bazaar was organized in 1839; special trains were run at reduced prices from Whitby and Pickering—these were probably the first railway excursions. Outside the west door of the church is a boulder of Shap Granite brought to the area by glacier movement.

1.8

THE BRIDESTONES

STARTING AND FINISHING POINT

Staindale car-park (94/101-883904). Take the Whitby road north from Thornton Dale, turning R after 1½ miles (2.5 km) onto Dalby Forest Drive (toll road). After 5½ miles (9 km) car-park on R at sharp bend.

LENGTH

3 miles (5 km)

ASCENT

325 feet (100 m)

The High and Low Bridestones are two series of rock outcrops which stand on open heather moorland owned by the National Trust. They have been carved by the wind and rain into unusual shapes. One of the stones, weighing many tons, stands on a narrow base. The approach to the stones is past Staindale Water and along the National Trust nature trail. The walk passes through mixed woodland offering an interesting variety of scenery in a very short distance.

ROUTE DESCRIPTION (Map 12)

From the car-park follow the stream towards the lake *(1)* and turn R around the shore. The path climbs slightly to join a gravel

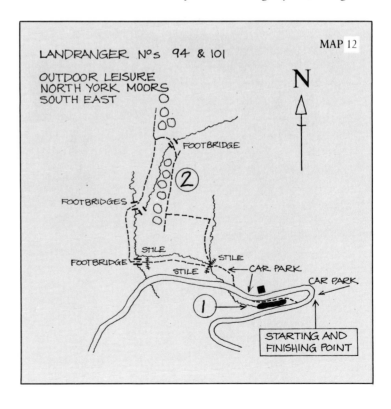

path beside the toll road. Pass the toilets, turn half R across the car-park and follow the path to a National Trust Omega sign and two stiles. Pass over the stile on your R and into the wood.

The path climbs steeply through mixed woodland with a stream on the R. At the top of the hill there is a convenient seat offering a lovely view of the woodland. Follow the path which reaches open moorland and turn L at a yellow waymark arrow. Follow the track across the bracken and heather-covered moor to the Low Bridestones which appear on the skyline. Turn R at the first of the stones and follow the path passing about eight rock outcrops (2).

Your path then descends into Bridestones Griff, a small stream fringed by trees, and sweeps back up the hillside to the High Bridestones. Take the path to the R to see all the Bridestones then return to the junction. Carry straight on along the ridge (i.e. to the L at the junction from your original direction) which offers views on your L, across the valley, to the Low Bridestones. The path eventually descends to a stream. Cross the footbridge on your R and follow the moorland valley keeping the stream on your L. A footbridge crosses the stream and leads to a stile into a field. The path swings L, following the edge of the wood to a stile. Bear half R down to the car-park you crossed earlier and retrace your steps around the lake back to the car-park.

1 *Staindale Water*
   This lake was created only a few years ago to attract a greater variety of wildlife to the area. You may see Canada geese, tufted duck or mallard on the lake and crossbills and siskin in the surrounding woodlands.

2 *The Bridestones*
   The Low Bridestones are the first group of rock outcrops encountered on the walk, the High Bridestones are to the north across Bridestones Griff. The fantastically shaped rocks have been sculptured by wind and water over some 60,000 years. The harder siliceous sandstone has resisted the erosion better than the less durable calcerous sandstone which has been washed away.

The Low Bridestones

FARNDALE'S DAFFODIL WALK

This pleasant summer walk becomes a major tourist attraction in April when the wild daffodils bloom. A one-way system then operates on the narrow dales roads and extra fields are available for parking. Once on the walk and away from the traffic you will be able to enjoy the beauty of the daffodils and the rugged valley of Farndale.

ROUTE DESCRIPTION (Map 13)

From the car-park at Low Mill *(1)* take the path through the small gate (PFS to Church Houses) near the entrance. Walk down the paved way, cross over the footbridge and turn L. Follow the distinct path beside the River Dove for the next mile (1.6 km) *(2)*. The path eventually passes between a group of buildings *(3)* and bears R through a gate and on to Church Houses. Turn R and R again at the next two road junctions, then continue up the hill passing the church on your L. *(4)*.

Turn R 600 yards (550 m) beyond the last junction through a gate, keeping the wall on your L, to a stile. The next section sounds complicated, but the route is well signposted. Turn L over the stile and follow the hedge to a gate then continue above

Farndale churchyard

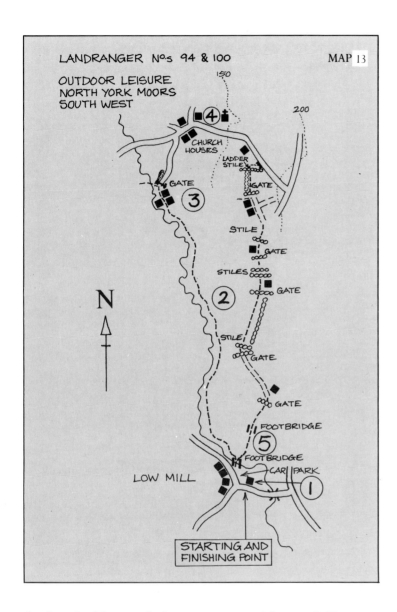

the farm buildings and along an access road. Bear half R (PFS) across the field to a stone stile and continue above Bitchagreen Farm. Pass through a gate and cross the field to a stile and then continue to a ladder stile. Bear half R over the field to a gate and continue on a paved way with a hedge on your L. Turn L at the stile and gate and cross the field into a farm lane. Turn R through a gate in the farmyard which leads to a stile and bridge over a stream; a paved way crosses the field *(5)* to the footbridge, which leads back to the car-park in Low Mill.

1 Low Mill
The hamlet takes its name from the water-powered mill erected in the middle of the nineteenth century. It ground

Banks of the River Dove

corn until the 1930s and was used to generate electricity until 1956. The building has now been altered, but the leat along which the water was brought to power the mill can still be seen beside the River Dove.

2 *Wild Daffodils*

The banks of the River Dove offer a fine display of the wild daffodil (*Narcissus pseudonarcissus*), a native British plant. It has been dispersed along the river banks by various floods and can be found for about six miles (9.5 km). This is a nature reserve and it is an offence to pick or damage the plants.

3 *High Mill, Church Houses*

As you reach the buildings you pass two huge stone gateposts; one bears the inscription 'IG, IWF, JS, 1826'. The building on the R was a blacksmith's shop which was worked by James Kneeshaw in the 1890s. The next building was the corn mill powered by an overshot wheel receiving its water from Blakey Gill, a side stream of the River Dove. In the 1890s the miller was Mrs Ann Garbutt, but the mill ceased working about ten years later. The mill wheel and equipment were still in place ten years ago.

4 *Farndale Church*

The church was built in 1831 on the site of an earlier church. It was restored between 1907 and 1914, when the west front was added. The churchyard contains a good display of daffodils in the season, probably transplanted over many years by local people.

5 *Paved ways*   See page 56.

2.10

A SHIPWRECK TRAIL

STARTING POINT
Lifeboat Museum, Whitby (94-898114).
FINISHING POINT
The Dock, Robin Hood's Bay (94-953048).
LENGTH
7 miles (11 km)
ASCENT
500 feet (150 m)

The Lifeboat Museum in Whitby contains one of the last rowing lifeboats and items from numerous wrecks along this stretch of coast. Many lives have been lost, but given a fighting chance these local people would wrestle victory from disaster. The walk keeps to the cliff-top path with easy route-finding and fine views. The walk ends in the interesting village of Robin Hood's Bay with its crowded collection of stone cottages.

ROUTE DESCRIPTION (Maps 14, 15)

From the Lifeboat Museum turn R upstream and cross the swing bridge over the River Esk. Take the second turn L along Church Street to the 199 Steps (1). Ascend the steps passing Caedmon Cross (2) at the top to the parish church (3). Continue on, out of the churchyard, to a car-park with Whitby Abbey (4) on your R. Turn L across the car-park and head for the base of the television transmitter. A path passes it on the seaward side and continues south along the cliff-top path.

As you approach Saltwick Nab you pass the scene of the *Rohilla* disaster (5), which brought about acts of heroism rarely surpassed. The path leads into a holiday village. Continue on the road between the buildings and pick up the cliff-top path just beyond the entrance to the site. To the L is a rock tooth sticking out of the sea. This was the site of one of the most recent wrecks, when the Scarborough fishing boat *Admiral Von Tromp* ran ashore. The path passes on the seaward side of Whitby fog horn, then passes inland around the lighthouse and afterwards rejoins the cliff-top path.

Continue south on the cliff top (6) to North Cheek. The Cheek was the scene of the shipwreck of the *Heatherfield* (7). From this point Robin Hood's Bay begins to open out but Bay Town remains hidden until the last moment. Eventually turn R at a small gate PFS, cross a short footbridge, and you are soon passing houses and entering Mount Pleasant North. At the end of the road turn L down to the car-park on the cliff top. As you begin to descend into the village you have a fine view over the

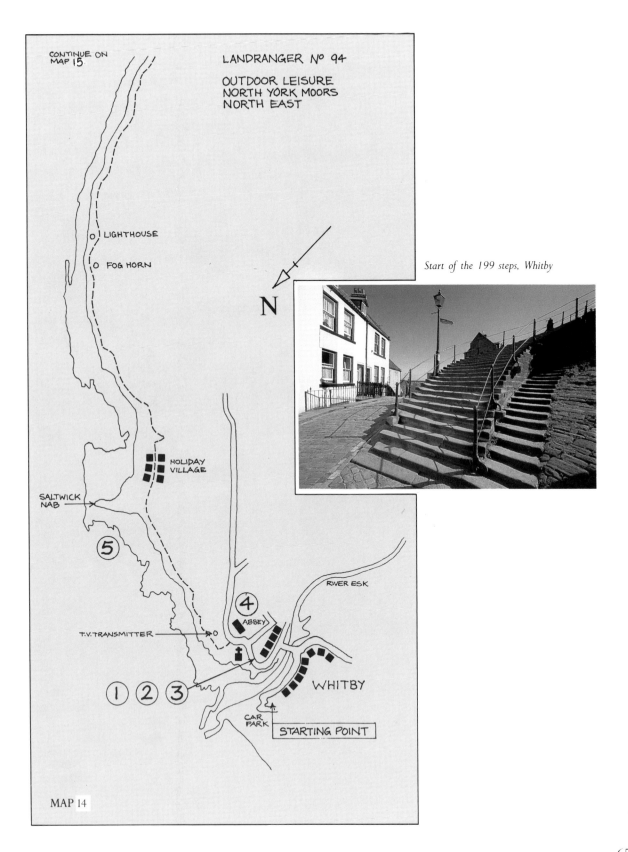

LANDRANGER Nº 94

OUTDOOR LEISURE
NORTH YORK MOORS
NORTH EAST

O | LIGHTHOUSE

O | FOG HORN

N

Start of the 199 steps, Whitby

HOLIDAY
VILLAGE

SALTWICK
NAB

⑤

RIVER ESK

④

ABBEY

T.V. TRANSMITTER → O

① ② ③

WHITBY

CAR
PARK

STARTING POINT

MAP 14

65

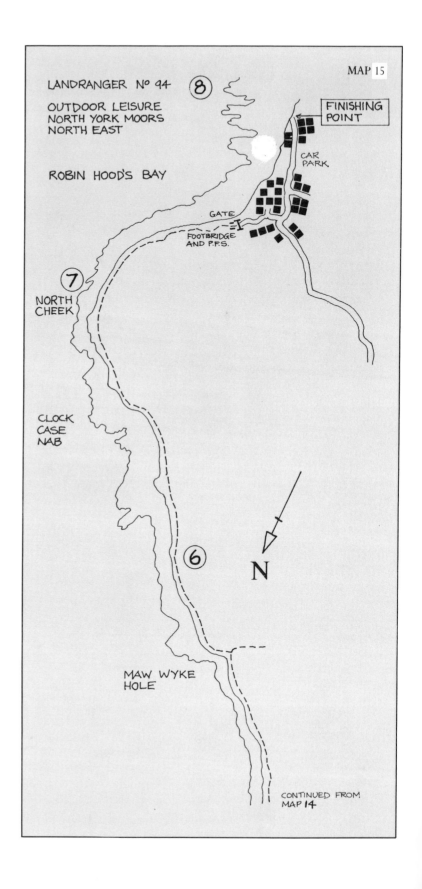

MAP 15

LANDRANGER Nº 94

OUTDOOR LEISURE
NORTH YORK MOORS
NORTH EAST

ROBIN HOOD'S BAY

⑧

FINISHING
POINT

CAR
PARK

GATE

FOOTBRIDGE
AND P.F.S.

⑦

NORTH
CHEEK

CLOCK
CASE
NAB

⑥

N

MAW WYKE
HOLE

CONTINUED FROM
MAP 14

house-tops into Robin Hood's Bay *(8)*. The road descends steeply into Bay Town turning R at the Laurel Inn, then turn L after the bridge to reach the slipway down to the beach. You have to return to the car-park at the top of the cliff for transport, but explore the many passageways in this interesting village on the way back.

1 *199 steps*

Count them—they have been worn over the years by people climbing to their cliff-top church. To the right of the steps is the old cobbled carriageway for horsedrawn traffic to Abbey House.

2 *Caedmon Cross*

The 20 feet (6 m) sandstone cross commemorates Caedmon, a lay brother at Whitby Abbey. After a dream he began to compose sacred verse and is acknowledged as the father of English sacred music.

3 *Whitby parish church*

The church has an interesting and unusual interior. It still contains box pews, some bearing the names of nearby villages who used them. Beside the pulpit is an ear trumpet for the use of a former minister's deaf wife. The interior was built in 1612 by local shipwrights and resembles the interior of a ship.

4 *Whitby Abbey*

The original abbey on this site was the setting for the Synod of Whitby in 664, which fixed the date of Easter. The present ruins are in the Early English style with a few Decorated windows. The nave collapsed during a storm in 1763 and the central tower in 1830. Further damage was sustained during the bombardment of Whitby by German warships in 1914.

5 The Rohilla *disaster*

On 30 October 1914 the hospital ship *Rohilla* was believed to have struck a mine and ran aground on Saltwick Nab with 229 people on board. The Whitby lifeboat couldn't be rowed out of the harbour due to a gale, so they dragged it on its carriage along the foot of the cliffs and launched it near the wreck. At the first attempt they rescued seventeen people. The lifeboat was swept along the coast, but it was dragged back for a second attempt and eighteen lives were saved. The lifeboat was then smashed against the cliffs by the rising tide. The Upgang lifeboat was lowered down the cliff but the high tide prevented the boat from being launched. A tug from Hartlepool attempted to get Whitby's second lifeboat to the scene but failed. Teesmouth's motor lifeboat was summoned but was disabled and had to return to port. Scarborough's

Caedmon Cross and Whitby Parish Church

lifeboat was towed to the scene by a tug, but due to the storm and after sixteen hours at sea the exhausted crew failed to get close. Eventually the Tynemouth motor lifeboat battled forty-four miles (71 km) down the coast and managed to get alongside. In fifty hours, with the use of six lifeboats, they had saved 85 lives, and a further sixty people had been washed ashore alive. The RNLI issued three gold medals and four silver medals for outstanding heroism.

6 *The Cleveland Way and Coast to Coast Walk*

The whole walk is along part of the Cleveland Way. At Maw Wyke Hole the path is used by walkers on Alfred Wainwright's Coast to Coast Walk. They are at the end of a 190-mile (306-km) walk from St Bees Head in Cumbria to Robin Hood's Bay.

7 Heatherfield *shipwreck*

On 26 January 1936 the 500-ton (492-tonne) coaster *Heatherfield* ran ashore on North Cheek in fog. The rocket brigade fired lines from the cliff top and the second shot straddled the ship 200 yards (180 m) off shore. The crew were taken off by breeches buoy.

8 *The* Visitor *shipwreck*

The bay was the scene of a dramatic rescue in 1881 of the crew of the brig *Visitor*. At 8.00 a.m. on 18 January the people of Bay Town witnessed the sinking of the ship. Six of the crew had taken to a boat and were sheltering from the storm in the lee of the wreck. The Whitby lifeboat couldn't get out of the harbour due to the storm so it was decided to take it to the bay by land. The roads were covered up to a depth of seven feet (2 m) in snow but sixty men started digging through the drifts from Whitby while folk from Bay Town started digging to meet them. Eleven horses and 200 men manhandled the boat out of Whitby and over the moor top. The lifeboat was lowered into the village, passing the corner at the Laurel Inn with only inches to spare, to be launched to the wreck. At the first attempt the furious sea smashed six oars, at the second attempt a crew of eighteen battled through the storm to rescue the survivors.

Whitby harbour

The Captain Cook Circuit

STARTING AND FINISHING POINT
The Captain Cook Museum, Great Ayton (93-561107).
LENGTH
7½ miles (12 km)
ASCENT
1350 feet (410 m)

The walk starts from Great Ayton, where James Cook, the explorer, spent his childhood. The walk then climbs, steeply in places, to the summit of Easby Moor, where there is a monument to Cook. There are extensive views, including the peak of Roseberry Topping. After a moorland walk you ascend this fine view-point. The return to Great Ayton is made past Airy Holme Farm, where James Cook lived and his father worked.

Route Description (Maps 16, 17)

From the Captain Cook Museum *(1)* in Great Ayton, cross the road, turn R and cross over the footbridge. Fork L on the path by the weir to a gate. Bear half L along the distinct path, cross a stile and continue past a sports field on your R. The track bears half L across two fields, with the Cook Monument on the skyline, to a footbridge and a path that leads to a road. Turn R along the road into Little Ayton, turning L just before the bridge.

Walk up the road, pass through a gate, then skirt L around the farm buildings. Fork L up a broad track which crosses over a railway line. Continue to a T-junction, where you then turn R along a lane which rises steadily for ½ mile (800 m). When you reach the corner of a stone wall on your L turn L up to a gate into a forest. Turn half R and follow the path steeply up into the trees. Cross straight over a forest road and continue climbing with extensive views unfolding over the Cleveland Plain. As you reach the top and leave the trees the Captain Cook Monument *(2)* comes into view. On approaching the monument note the path on your L—this is your route of descent.

The view from the monument on a fine day extends to Marton, now part of Middlesbrough, where James Cook was born in 1728. Take the path across the moor you noted on your approach and continue down some steps; the path eventually becomes a broad track between the trees. When you reach the

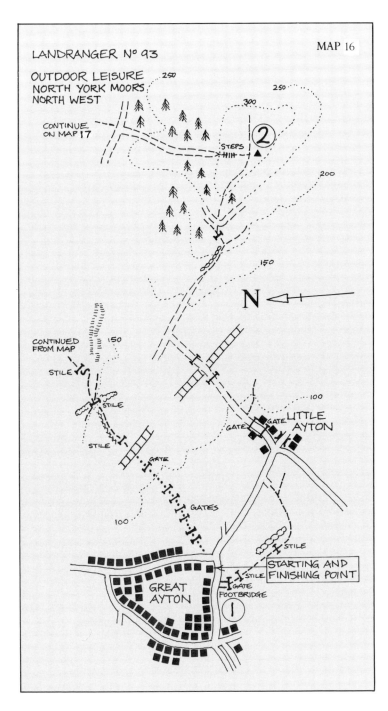

LANDRANGER Nº 93

OUTDOOR LEISURE
NORTH YORK MOORS
NORTH WEST

MAP 16

250

250

300

CONTINUE
ON MAP 17

STEPS

②

▲

200

150

N

CONTINUED
FROM MAP

150

STILE

STILE

STILE

100

GATE
GATE

LITTLE
AYTON

GATE

GATE

GATES

100

STILE

STARTING AND
FINISHING POINT

STILE

GREAT
AYTON

GATE
FOOTBRIDGE

①

road turn R for 50 yards (45 m) then turn L on the path which
climbs to Great Ayton Moor (Cleveland Way sign) *(3)*. Climb
the steps leading up beside the old stone wall and continue
along the edge of the moor with a stone wall on your L. Pass
through a gate, cross the col and climb steeply to the summit of
Roseberry Topping *(4)*.

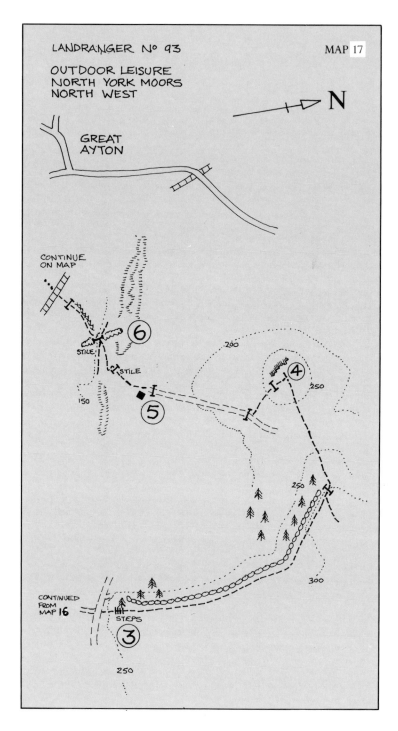

Be careful of your route of descent—there is a sheer cliff.
Retrace your steps from the summit for 30 yards (25 m) and
turn R down the hillside to a gate; walk down the field to join a
track and turn R through a gate. Follow the track to Airy Holme
Farm *(5)*. Turn R over a cattle grid (PFS) then half L across a

Captain Cook's school, Great Ayton

field to a stile to the L of a group of conifers. Turn L between the wire fences. There is a steep drop on your R where mining has taken place *(6)*. In 50 yards (45 m) turn R down a hillside; this is covered in bluebells each year in the late spring. Cross a track near a metal gate, descending to a stile, and after 20 yards (18 m) turn R alongside a wire fence to another stile.

Carry straight on with a hedge on your R, cross over a railway line and continue down the field through parkland. The path goes in a straight line passing through a number of metal gates until it reaches a road in Great Ayton. Turn L along the road, taking the second turn R back to the Captain Cook Museum.

1 Captain Cook Museum
The building was built in 1704 as a school at the expense of a local yeoman named Michael Postgate. It was to this school that James Cook came from nearby Airy Holme Farm. The cost of Cook's education was probably borne by Thomas Scottowe, Lord of the Manor of Ayton, who employed Cook's father as a hind or foreman. The school was rebuilt in 1785 and now contains a Cook Museum.

2 Captain Cook Monument
The monument, erected by Robert Campion of nearby Easby

Hall, overlooks Marton where the explorer was born and Great Ayton where he spent his childhood. The 51 foot (15.5 m) high memorial was completed on the centenary of Cook's birth on 27 October 1827. There is an inscription on three cast-iron panels on the monument.

3 *The Cleveland Way*

The 112 miles (180 km) Long Distance Footpath starts at Helmsley and heads west to Sutton Bank and Kilburn White Horse. The route then turns north to Osmotherley, over the Cleveland Hills and Roseberry Topping to the coast at Saltburn. For the last 52 miles (84 km) the cliff top path is followed, pasing through Whitby and Scarborough to finish at Filey Brigg.

4 *Roseberry Topping*

The hill offers an extremely fine view over Middlesbrough and along the coast. The steep crag to the west of the hill appeared when iron workings driven into the hill collapsed. The hill is close to where James Cook spent his boyhood and there is little doubt that someone as adventurous as Cook would have climbed this peak—probably gaining his first sight of the sea.

5 *Airy Holme Farm*

When James Cook was about seven his father moved from Marton to Airy Holme Farm to work as hind for Thomas Scottowe. When Cook's father retired he built a stone cottage in Great Ayton, beside the road to Easby. The cottage was shipped to Australia in 1933 and now stands in Fitzroy Gardens, Melbourne. An obelisk of stones from Point Hicks Hill, the first part of Australia sighted by Captain Cook, now stands on the site of the cottage.

6 *Whinstone mining*

Cutting across the North York Moors from a point north-east of Goathland to a point north of Great Ayton is the Cleveland Dyke. This narrow band of volcanic rock welled up out of the earth and solidified. As it is extremely hard, the whinstone has been quarried and used for surfacing roads.

Roseberry Topping from Easby Moor

THE FARNDALE HEAD CIRCUIT

STARTING AND FINISHING
POINT
Low Mill car-park, Farndale (94-673952). From Kirkbymoorside take the road to Gillamoor and continue on the Hutton-le-Hole road, turning L to Low Mill.
LENGTH
16 miles (26 km)
ASCENT
1000 feet (300 m)

This long walk is easy to follow once you have climbed out of Farndale and until you descend again into the valley. This leaves you free to enjoy the fine views from the ancient ridgeway and along the bed of the disused mineral railway.

ROUTE DESCRIPTION (Maps 18 – 21)

From the car-park turn R up the narrow road. After 400 yards (375 m) turn L over a cattle grid (PBS to Rudland Rigg). Walk up the track to Horn End Farm, at the junction of tracks walk straight on and pass through a gate. The track crosses the field to another gate then begins to swing R through more gates, eventually passing a stone barn on your L. Walk between the stone walls, pass through a gate, ignore the next gate and bear half L (PBS) on a track which leads to a footbridge.

After crossing the stream, walk up the field to a stile beside a gate. Follow the track which bears L but soon swings round to the R and climbs through the bracken onto Rudland Rigg *(1)*. Bear R along the ridge road; after 1½ miles (2.5 km) you pass the remains of Cockan Cross *(2)* and just over ½ mile (800 m) later the Cammon Stone *(3)*. Continue on the broad track to Bloworth Crossing *(4)* 1¼ miles (2 km) further on, where you reach a junction. At this remote point high on the moors turn R along the disused railway line. This is an easy way to traverse the moors as the mineral railway went into cuttings through the high ground and the streams are crossed on high embankments.

The rugged heights of Upper Farndale gradually descend into the head of the valley as you continue down the track, which has become popular with walkers *(5)*. After 3 miles (5 km) you pass a track to the L which descends to Esklets, a ruined farm near the source of the River Esk. You continue on the railway with Farndale *(6)* on the R for 2¾ miles (4.5 km) to Blakey Bank. As you approach Blakey Bank you pass close to the Lion Inn, which may be of interest during opening hours.

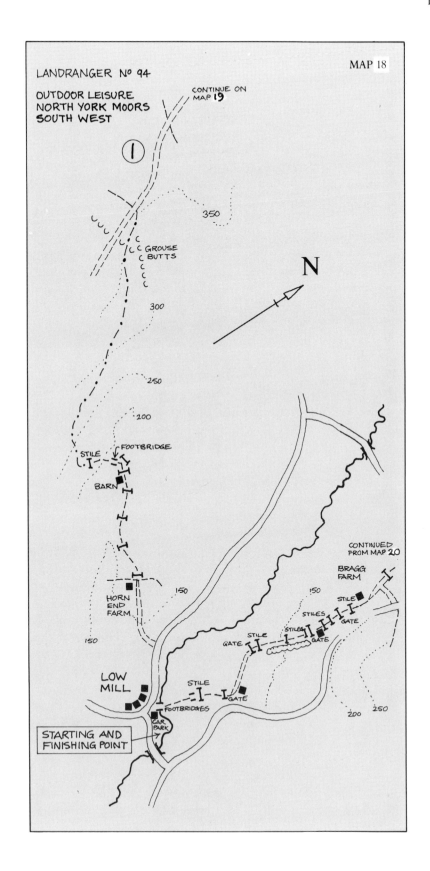

The Rudland Rigg Road

Approaching Blakey Bank the former railway passed through a tunnel under the road, but this is now blocked. Bear half R to the road, turn L to the junction and pick up the track opposite (PFS to Rosedale) then turn R on the railway going south *(7)*. Pass a 'Private no road' sign and continue down the track for a mile (1.6 km). To the L is an excellent view over Rosedale to East Mines. After a mile (1.6 km) turn R at a small cairn and pass the ruins of Sled Shoe House which are just visible from the railway track. An indistinct track leads across the heather moorland ridge to join the road near a line of shooting butts.

The indistinct path continues through the heather just to the north of the butts. A good view of Farndale opens up as you begin to descend into the dale. Head for a gate in a stone wall where a hollow way *(8)* leads down to the bottom of a field. Turn L, keeping the stone wall on your R and pass through a series of gates which lead to the road. Cross the road, take the lane opposite past the stone cottage and turn L at the PFS just before Bragg Farm.

The next section is well waymarked. Bear half R (PFS) across the field to a stone stile and continue above Bitchagreen Farm. Pass through a gate and cross the field to a stile and then continue to a ladder stile. Bear half R over a field to a gate and continue on a paved way with a hedge on your L. Turn R at the stile and gate and cross the field into a farm lane. Turn R through a gate in the farmyard, this leads to a stile and bridge over a stream. A paved way crosses the field to a footbridge which leads back to the car-park in Low Mill.

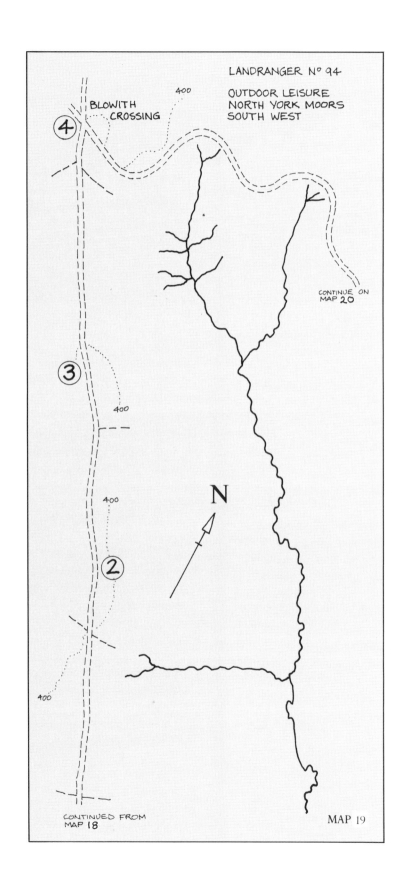

LANDRANGER N° 94

OUTDOOR LEISURE
NORTH YORK MOORS
SOUTH WEST

400

④ BLOWITH
····CROSSING

③

400

400

N

②

400

CONTINUE ON
MAP 20

CONTINUED FROM
MAP 18

MAP 19

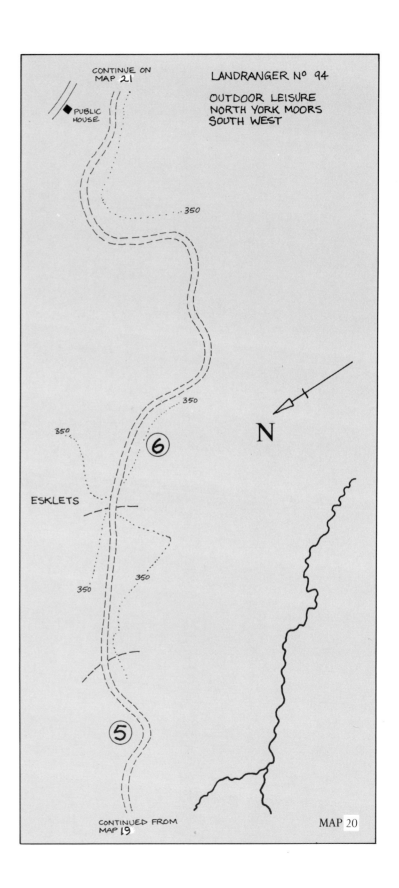

CONTINUE ON
MAP 21

LANDRANGER Nº 94

OUTDOOR LEISURE
NORTH YORK MOORS
SOUTH WEST

PUBLIC
HOUSE

350

N

350

6

ESKLETS

350

350

350

5

CONTINUED FROM
MAP 19

MAP 20

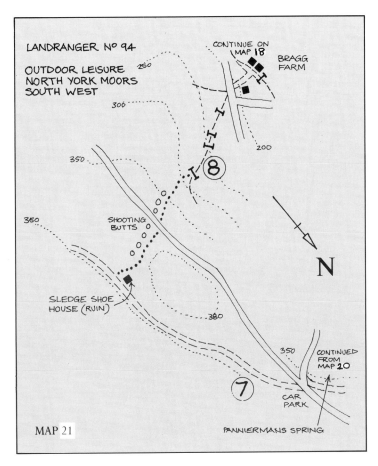

LANDRANGER N° 94

OUTDOOR LEISURE
NORTH YORK MOORS
SOUTH WEST

CONTINUE ON
MAP 18

BRAGG
FARM

250

306

350

350

SHOOTING
BUTTS

200

⑧

N

SLEDGE SHOE
HOUSE (RUIN)

380

350

CONTINUED
FROM
MAP 20

⑦

CAR
PARK

MAP 21

PANNIERMANS SPRING

1   Rudland Rigg

This ancient ridge route over the moors has probably been in use for 2,000 years. It would offer a reasonably dry north–south route over the rugged moors.

2   Cockan Cross

The broken shaft stands in a socket stone. The stone is inscribed 'Farndale; Stoxle Rode (Stokesley Road); Bransdale; Kirby Rode (Kirkbymoorside Road)'.

3   Cammon Stone

This large upright slab may have been erected as a waymarker in prehistoric times. There is a Hebrew inscription on the west side of the stone, placed there in more recent times.

4   Bloworth Crossing

This was the site of a level crossing on the Rosedale Ironstone Railway, which gives some indication of the amount of traffic on the road last century. It would be a hardy life for the crossing keeper and his family, 1200 feet (365 m) above sea level on these exposed moors.

5   Long distance walks

This ideal walking track is also used by walkers on the 40

mile (64 km) Lyke Wake Walk and the 190 mile (306 km) Coast to Coast Walk.

6 *Upper Farndale*

There have been plans put forward at various times since the 1930s to flood this part of the valley and create a reservoir, possibly turning the track into a road to bring in construction material. Fortunately the plans have so far been successfully resisted.

7 *Rosedale Ironstone Railway*

At this point the mineral railway split into two spurs, one heading north around the head of Rosedale to the East Mines which can be seen at the other side of the valley. Our route turned south to Sheriff's Pit and Rosedale Chimney.

8 *Hollow way*

These ancient tracks from the moors have been used for centuries to bring peat and goods into the village. The frequent use of these tracks has created a deep hollow below the level of the surrounding fields.

Farndale from Pannierman's Spring

1.13

BUTTERMERE

STARTING AND FINISHING
POINT
Buttermere Village. NPA car park
beside the Fish Hotel (NW-175169).
LENGTH
4 miles (6.4 km)
ASCENT
50 ft (15 m)

The quintessence of natural beauty—or so thought the tourists of the nineteenth century. Many today still regard Buttermere—'the lake by the dairy pastures'—as the prettiest of the smaller lakes. A footpath circuits the shore, making it an easy and delightful family walking area. Large sections of this walk are well sheltered—either by trees or, at one point, a rock tunnel!—making it a good route for those days when poor weather renders the high fells inaccessible.

ROUTE DESCRIPTION (Map 22)

Walk back to the car park entrance and bear R, around the front of the Fish Hotel (1), to a track (PBS 'Buttermere Lake, Scale Bridge'). Turn R and follow the track for 200 yards (182 m) until you arrive at a farm gate and a fork in the track. Keep L, through a kissing gate and between the fields. Directly in front of you is a waterfall, tumbling down from Bleaberry Tarn; this is Sourmilk Gill (a popular name for Lake District waterfalls—you will encounter two more Sourmilk Gill's during the course of routes elsewhere in this book).

Arriving at another farm gate, cross the stile alongside and continue across the fields to a footbridge. Cross the beck and the path forks again; bear L, along the lake shore towards the trees. As you enter the wood, there is a path on your R, signed Scale Force. Keep L, across a second footbridge and through a kissing gate, into Burtness Wood. After a few yards you will pass another path going up through the trees on your R, to Red Pike. Ignore it and carry straight on, walking along a level, well-made bridle track. This is a lovely path through the woods, walking R along the shore line, with views across the lake to Goat Crag.

After $\frac{1}{2}$ mile (0.8 km), the track appears to split three ways; take the narrower, L-hand path, across a footbridge (a pair of railway sleepers) and continue along the shore. You come to a superb view of Fleetwith Pike. The path meanders along the shore for another 400 yards (364 m) and brings you to a stone

Sheep at Gatesgarth Farm

wall and a kissing gate. Once through, you leave the woods behind and have open fellside on your R, covered with bracken. As you approach the head of the lake, you are joined on your L by a drystone wall. Follow this until you pass a sheep enclosure and arrive at a junction. The path to your R climbs up to Scarth Gap and Haystacks. Go L, though a kissing gate and across a footbridge to follow the track across the fields to Gatesgarth Farm. The track bears L to Gatesgarth Beck and then through a narrow gate, to skirt round to the L of the farmyard and bring you out onto the Honister Pass road.

Turn L and follow the road for 500 yards (455 m) until you return to the lake shore and a narrow, permissive path off to your L. Follow the path to a kissing gate and continue along the shore, through two fields. As you draw closer to a wood, the shore becomes littered with pebbles and it becomes difficult to resist the temptation to try skimming the odd stone across the surface of the lake.

Go through a kissing gate into the woods and you are on a rough footpath which climbs the bank, above the level of the water. Suddenly you find yourself confronted by a tunnel, blasted through the rocks in front of you *(2)*.

Follow the path through the tunnel for 40 yards (36 m) (be warned—the roof is low in places) and you emerge back into daylight on a more level, easily negotiated path. The footpath is now well-defined and straightforward to follow. It leads you through the woods and back out onto fields. You re-enter another small wood. After a quarter-of-a-mile, you come to a

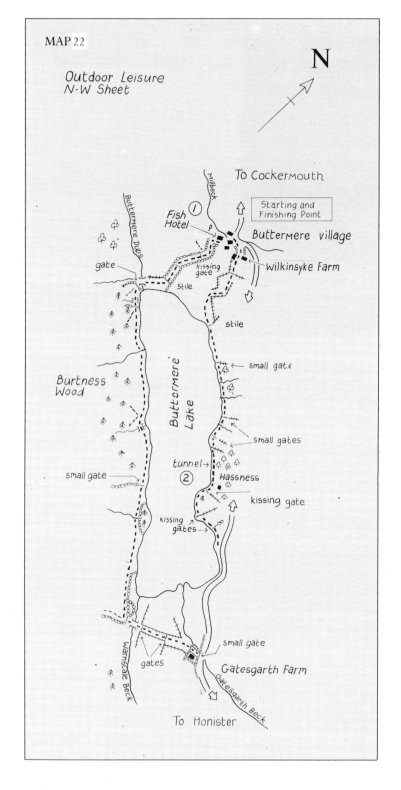

MAP 22

Outdoor Leisure
N-W Sheet

N

To Cockermouth

Starting and
Finishing Point

Milbeck

Fish
Hotel ①

P

Buttermere village

Buttermere Dubs

gate

kissing
gate

Wilkinsyke Farm

stile

stile

small gate

Burtness
Wood

Buttermere Lake

small gates

tunnel →

② Hassness

small gate

kissing gate

kissing
gates →

Wamscale Beck

gates

small gate

Gatesgarth Farm

Gatesgarth Beck

To Honister

View of High Crag, High Stile and Red Pike from Lower Gatesgarth

wire fence and a stile. Cross over and follow the path through another field until you arrive at a small gate. Go through and bear R along a track. This brings you to Wilkinsyke Farm. Go through the farmyard and out onto the main road. Turn L and follow the road back into Buttermere village.

1 The Fish Hotel

Originally The Fish Inn, this was a scene of some excitement in the early years of the nineteenth century when it became the centre of an outrageous scandal. It was the home of Mary Robinson, whose father owned the Inn. A renowned local beauty, her charms were praised by the eccentric writer and traveller, Joseph Budworth, in his *A Fortnight's Ramble in the Lakes*, published in 1792.

Ten years later, the Inn was visited by a gentleman calling himself the Honourable Colonel Alexander Augustus Hope, MP, who came in search of char fishing but caught Mary instead. After a whirlwind romance, during which everyone applauded Mary's good fortune, he married her. The affair was reported in the London *Morning Post*, by their correspondent, Samuel Taylor Coleridge. Once his article appeared, the fun started: Hope's brother, Charles, Earl of Hopetown, expressed grave doubts about the authenticity of the groom as his brother was at that time travelling in Europe. An outcry followed and upon his return from their honeymoon in Scotland, Hope was arrested and unmasked as James Hatfield, a swindler and bigamist. In the midst of the ensuing uproar, Hatfield seems to have coolly bluffed his way onto a fishing trip and escaped across the lake. He was captured, two months later, in Wales and tried in Carlisle. Widespread public sympathy for Mary, who by then was with child, resulted in Hatfield's execution by hanging in 1803.

The story of the 'Keswick Imposter' became the currency of novelists and playwrights for the next century. Charles Lamb reported seeing a highly coloured version of the affair upon the London stage.

Mary later married a local farmer and she now lies buried in Caldbeck churchyard.

2 The Buttermere Tunnel

George Benson, the nineteenth-century owner of nearby Hassness House, is credited with the creation of this unusual feature. There are two theories why he had the tunnel built; one states that he was irritated at not being able to walk the entire circumference of the lake upon the shore; the other suggests that he had the tunnel blasted through the rocks to keep his workmen busy during idle winter months.

Group of conifers just south of Burtness Wood by the shores of Buttermere

1.14

R<small>YDAL</small> W<small>ATER</small>

STARTING AND FINISHING
POINT
N<small>PA</small> car park at Pelter Bridge, along a
small lane just off the A591
(S<small>E</small>-364062)
LENGTH
$3\frac{3}{4}$ miles (6 km)
ASCENT
250 ft (75 m)

An attractive, reedy lake, all too easily passed by those hurrying along the road in search of the delights of Grasmere. The southern shore is the special preserve of the walker. A complete circuit—using the old coffin track between Town End and Rydal Mount—makes a very enjoyable family walk.

R<small>OUTE</small> D<small>ESCRIPTION</small> (Map 23)

From the car park turn L along the minor road, following the lane uphill, past two tiny rows of terraced cottages. After 400 yards (364 m) you pass through a gap alongside a farm gate and the lane deteriorates to a muddy track. The route descends to another farm gate. Go through the small gate alongside and you find yourself beside Rydal Water.

The path forks as soon as you come through the gate. The R-hand path takes you down to the lake and a route which meanders along the lake shore. Go L, uphill to a small wooden bench and a good view over the lake. Directly in front of you, on the far side of the lake, is Nab Scar and below the crag, by the road, is a white cottage *(1)*.

Continue along the path, crossing a small beck and bearing L to climb up into the trees. As the stone wall on your right gives out, you can detour L slightly to avoid a stretch of rough ground. Then bear R again (beware a faint track off to your L, through the bracken) to join the track where the wall resumes. Continue uphill to an old slate quarry. You will pass a cave on your L. Although safe to explore, there is quite a scramble to enter it.

Follow the path past the cave and you start to climb a steep-sided slate tip. This brings you out onto a wide plateau and, in front of you, another, larger cave *(2)*.

Bear R across the plateau and over a small incline, disregarding a path on your L. Passing another bench, you walk downhill again along a clearly defined path. Ahead of you is White Moss Common. Bear around to the L of a group of conifers, following the bracken-covered flanks of Loughrigg Fell.

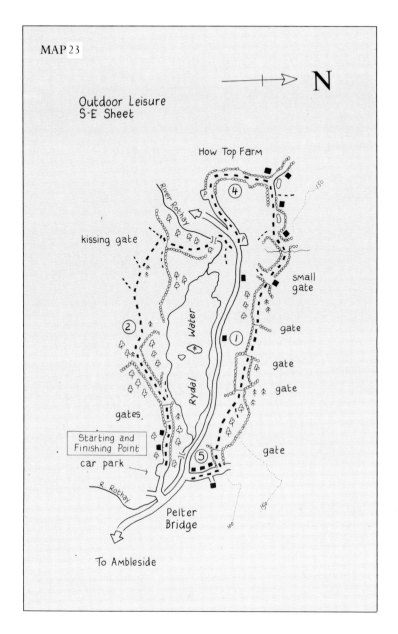

MAP 23

N

Outdoor Leisure
S-E Sheet

How Top Farm

④

River Rothay

kissing gate

small
gate

②

Rydal Water

gate

①

gate

gate

gates.

Starting and
Finishing Point

car park ➔

⑤

gate

R. Rothay

Pelter
Bridge

To Ambleside

Just beyond the trees, the path forks, the L-hand path taking
you up onto Loughrigg Terrace. Bear half-R and follow the path
up onto a small ridge, overlooking the river which links
Grasmere Lake and Rydal Water. Ahead of you, across
Grasmere, is Helm Crag (3).

At the ridge, turn R and follow the path downhill to a kissing
gate in the stone wall on your L. Go through and you are in a
pleasant, mixed woodland. The path is heavily eroded and

*Rydal Water used to be called Routhermere or Rothaymere after the river which
flows through it*

therefore easy to follow. It winds downhill through the trees and brings you to a long wooden footbridge across the river. Once you have crossed, turn R and follow the river until you arrive at a fork in the path. Bear L and the path climbs uphill to the main road.

Cross the road and bear L through White Moss car park. There is a road ahead of you which goes up onto White Moss Common—and, invariably, in summer an ice cream van standing at the junction of this minor road and the A591. Follow the minor road uphill.

Follow the road for perhaps a $\frac{1}{3}$ mile (0.5 km) and you will pass a grove of trees on your R. There is a path which detours through the tree to a wooden bench and a grand view of Grasmere Lake *(4)* before rejoining the road a few hundred yards farther on.

Continue along the road until the junction at How Top Farm. Turn R (there is a slate sign by the road marked 'Footpath to Rydal') and continue up the hill, passing a sign on your L for Alcock Tarn. The road continues past a small pond and then peters out to a rough track. Ignore the path on your R which climbs over White Moss Common. The track winds round to the R, over Dunney Beck and passes just below a house called Brockstone. Once again, ignore a footpath on your R and continue through a small gate and along the track.

The track can be rough in places but it is straightforward walking. You follow the line of the wall on your R, past a stone embankment in the fellside, and through another gate in the stone wall on your R. This takes you through trees with glimpses of scree on the fellside above you. After 300 yards (273 m), you pass through another gate in a stone wall ahead of you and walk across a succession of fields, keeping to the clearly-defined track the whole time. On your right you start to have a clear view over Rydal Water.

After $\frac{1}{2}$ mile (0.8 km) you pass through a farm gate and the track leads between two stone walls to emerge onto a tarmac road. Turn R and walk downhill, past Rydal Mount *(5)*.

This quiet lane leads down to the A591 again. Turn L and follow the road for 300 yards (273 m) until you come opposite Peler Bridge. Cross the road and walk back to the car park.

1 Nab Cottage

Originally Nab Farm, this house was the home of Margaret Simpson who was courted and later married by Thomas De' Quincey. In 1829 he bought the house from her father and moved to the farm.

De Quincey first came to the Lake District in 1805,

making a pilgrimage to see his great idol, Wordsworth. His nerve failed him, however, and he returned to university at Oxford, having only got as far as Coniston. In April the following year, he tried again; the following August he actually got close enough to see Dove Cottage! He finally made it in 1807, accompanying Coleridge's wife, Sara, on the long journey from the West Country to Grasmere. He stayed several months and when Wordsworth moved to Allan Bank, he took over the tenancy.

It was here that he achieved notoriety as the author of *Confessions of an English Opium Eater*, first published in *London Magazine* in 1821. Even before this time, Wordsworth seems to have treated him badly, even writing to De Quincey's mother to urge her to put a stop to this unsuitable liaison with a farmer's daughter. De Quincey kept on the tenancy of Dove Cottage for ten years after moving to the Nab, mainly to store his vast wealth of books. He later got his own back on Wordsworth and his circle with a wonderful collection of scurrilous memories, entitled *Recollections of the Lakes and the Lake Poets.*

2 *Rydal Caves*

These caves—caused by slate quarrying—have now become an accepted feature of the local landscape. The second of them is the larger—the roof is nearly 40 feet (12 m) high—and has served over the years as picnic site, rain shelter, camp site and even concert hall; students from Charlotte Mason College in Ambleside frequently sing carols here just prior to the Christmas vacation.

3 *Helm Crag*

This craggy summit stands to the north of the village and is known variously as 'The Lion and the Lamb' and 'The Old Woman on the Organ', because of the fantastic shapes which are formed by the rocks on the summit. One nineteenth-century writer was so impressed that he even claimed that Helm Crag was the shell of an extinct volcano.

4 *John's Grove*

William and Dorothy Wordsworth had their own pet names for much of the landscape around Grasmere and Rydal. One such was John's Grove, the short stretch of woodland which commands such a fine view of the lake and island. They named it after their brother, John, a captain in the merchant navy, who would sometimes pace up and down this grove, as if on the deck of his ship. He died when his ship, *The Earl of Abergavenny* went down off Portland Bill in storms in 1805. Over 300 crew and passengers perished and the newspapers of the day regarded it as a national catastrophe.

Cave near Rydal Water

5 *Rydal Mount*

Wordsworth's home from 1813 until his death in 1850. He moved here to escape the unhappy associations of Grasmere vale, following the deaths of his two youngest children. By this time, Wordsworth was past his best as a poet and the radical reformer of his youth had given way to a somewhat staid member of the establishment of the day. He became a kind of civil servant—Distributor of Stamps for Westmorland—and, in 1843, was appointed Poet Laureate, following the death of his old friend, Robert Southey. A much grander house than Dove Cottage, it became a popular tourist attraction, even during the poet's lifetime. The house is now open to the public.

A short distance down the road is the Church of St Mary, built by Lady Ann Fleming (Wordsworth's landlady) in 1824. Wordsworth was chapel warden in 1833. Behind the church lies Dora's Field, now owned by the National Trust. It was originally purchased by Wordsworth with the intention of building a home there, should he ever leave Rydal Mount (Wordsworth did not own any of the houses he lived in). He eventually gave it to his daughter, Dora, and each Spring it boasts a beautiful display of daffodils.

ULLSWATER

Park at Glenridding and catch the
launch to Howtown. The walk starts
from Howtown Pier (NE-444198) and
finishes back at Glenridding.
LENGTH
6½ miles (10.4 km)
ASCENT
395 ft (120 m)

The tree-lined eastern shores of Ullswater provide the setting
for this walk from Howtown to Glenridding. Undisturbed by
roads or traffic, this is one of the best low-level routes you will
encounter in the Lake District. The start of the walk is
approached by a launch from Glenridding, a very pleasant way
to survey the footpath before you begin.

ROUTE DESCRIPTION (Maps 24, 25)

Howtown stands beside a bay, overlooked by Hallin Fell and the
northern slopes of High Street. The launch *(1)* will tie alongside
a wooden pier which leads you into a group of trees and over a
tiny footbridge. Immediately you have crossed the beck, turn L
and go through a fence and along the lake shore. If you have
caught the first launch on a summer Sunday, you will have to
put on a burst of speed at this point to overtake the crowds.
Follow the shoreline around the bay and through a kissing gate.
At a second kissing gate, turn R along a farm track, continuing
along the shore. You will come to a farm gate and another
kissing gate (PFS 'Patterdale, Sandwick'). Go through, following
the stone wall on your R and up a series of steps to yet a further
kissing gate. Go through and turn R, following a clear track
around the side of Hallin Fell.

As you walk past the trees on your R, the view opens out and
you are looking across the bay and along Ullswater *(2)*. After ½
mile (0.8 km), you have climbed perhaps 150 feet (45 m) above
the lake. You follow the path around Geordie's Crag and then it
descends again into the trees. You are now walking through
mixed, mainly deciduous woodland, right on the lake shore. The
path becomes rough underfoot in parts and brings you down
onto a rocky beach before re-entering the woods. You walk
around the L of a small wooded knoll and begin to climb again
along a well-made path through the trees, still keeping just
above the shoreline.

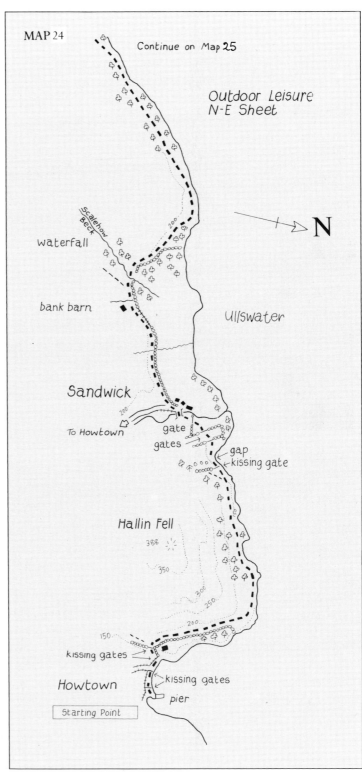

Near Sandwick on the shore of Ullswater

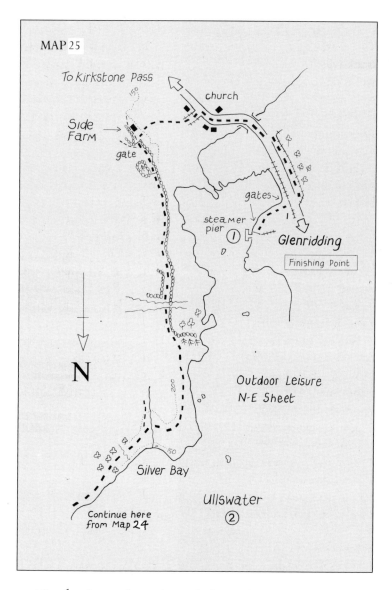

After $\frac{1}{2}$ mile (0.8 km), the path descends to a kissing gate in a drystone wall (notice the log and chain closing mechanism on the gate). Twenty yards (18 m) farther on you pass through a gap in an old stone wall and the path leads you down onto open fields, leaving the trees behind you. The footpath goes straight across the field to a gate in a stone wall, whilst the shore line curves round to your R. As you walk across the field you will pass a signpost, indicating Howtown and Sandwick. Go across a second field to another gate and then bear L, across the third field, towards trees and another gate. This brings you into another field, alongside a stream. Follow the path and you cross a bridge and enter the tiny hamlet of Sandwick.

Turn L up the tarmac road for 100 yards (91 m) until you

pass the last of the attractive cottages on your R (the last one is Townend Cottage), then leave the road and turn R onto a grass track (PFS 'Patterdale'). The track goes steeply uphill for a few yards, then becomes level once more and follows the drystone wall on your right. You are now moving away from the lake shore and, as the wall becomes a fence, you have a view to fields sweeping down to the tree-lined shore. Ahead of you and to the R is Birk Fell.

Half a mile (0.8 km) along the wall you will pass a bank barn and come to a small beck. Cross and, where the path forks, bear half-R. The track descends to Scalehow Beck.

At this point you can make a worthwhile detour up the fellside on your L to an attractive, tree-lined waterfall.

Following the track once more, you go uphill again and eventually leave the stone wall behind and the view opens out. Across the lake you can see Gowbarrow Park (3). A mile (1.6 km) of rough, undulating track now winds above the shore, through trees and bracken, around to Silver Bay.

As you leave the trees, the track forks. Bear R, around the bay, and as you climb up past Silver Point you are greeted by a view of Glenridding. Follow the track and you will come to a ridge lined with tall conifers. After crossing two small becks, you start to walk between two stone walls until, after 200 yards (182 m), the enclosure on your L ends and you have open, bracken-covered fellside above you.

You begin a slow, gradual descent towards Side Farm (there is a campsite on the R). Disregard a couple of paths on your L as you approach the farm. Once you reach Side Farm, the first thing you will probably want to do is buy an ice cream. Thus provisioned, turn R through the farmyard and follow the track across fields to the main road.

Turn R and follow the road. This section of the walk is a little dull, but there is no way to avoid it (unless you bully a companion into fetching the car). After a $\frac{1}{4}$ mile (0.4 km), cross the road at a bridge and continue for the same distance again until you come to a small path on your L. Bear L, up the narrow path for about 600 yards (546 m) until it drops back to the road. Cross over and through a gate to follow the lake shore around a field. This brings you back into the car park at Glenridding pier.

1 The Ullswater launches

There are two launches which sail the lake from Glenridding to Pooley Bridge, both run by the grandly-named Ullswater Navigation and Transit Company Limited. *Lady of the Lake* was first launched in 1877 and her sister ship, *Raven*, in 1889. Originally steam-driven, today they are powered by diesel.

The Company runs a regular daily service from Easter to the end of October.

2 *Ullswater*

The lake is second only to Windermere in length but far surpasses it for peace and solitude. Although a navigable highway, there are few motor-driven vessels on the lake, the speed boats and water skiers having been driven away by the 10mph speed restriction imposed in 1983. At the northern end of the lake there is an underground pumping station which draws off water to feed the reservoir at Haweswater.

3 *Gowbarrow Park*

It was on April 15, 1802, whilst walking through Gowbarrow Wood to visit their friends the Clarksons, at Eusemere, that William and Dorothy Wordsworth came upon a bank of daffodils. Later, Dorothy noted in her Journal: 'I never saw daffodils so beautiful, they grew among the mossy stones about and about them, some resting their heads upon these stones as on a pillow for weariness and the rest tossed and reeled and danced and seemed as if they verily laughed with the wind that blew upon them over the lake, they looked so gay ever glancing ever changing.' Two years later, William used Dorothy's observations as the basis of a poem and the 'host of golden daffodils' passed into the realm of literature.

Gowbarrow Park is now owned by the National Trust. The castellated tower you can glimpse above the tree tops is Lyulph's Tower, originally a hunting lodge built in the early 1800s by the Duke of Norfolk. The name—and that of the lake itself—is thought to derive from an early Norse settler, the first Lord of Ullswater.

Herdwick sheep near Sandwick

2.16

BLENCATHRA

STARTING AND FINISHING
POINT
A tiny car park along the minor road,
just past the White Horse Inn
(NE-348273), near Scales on the A66
(Penrith—Cockermouth road)
LENGTH
5½ miles (8.8 km)
ASCENT
2180 ft (660 m)

Sometimes called Saddleback—a sad example of dereliction of
the English language—Blencathra lacks Skiddaw's popularity
but has more character. This walk is straightforward until you
ascend Sharp Edge. This is a prominent arête which towers over
Scales Tarn and can leave you feeling exposed and vulnerable.
Consult your nerves before setting out (and be honest).

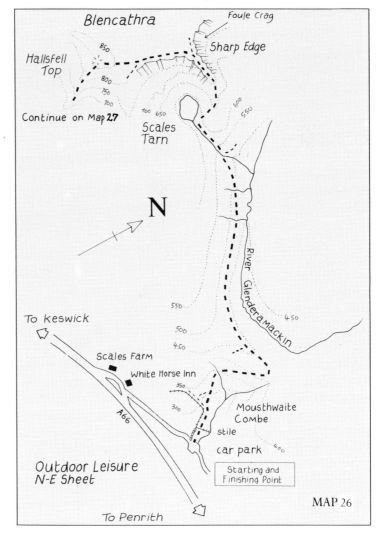

Blencathra

Foule Crag

Sharp Edge

Hallsfell
Top

Continue on Map 2.7

Scales
Tarn

N

River Glenderamackin

To keswick

Scales Farm

White Horse Inn

Mousthwaite
Combe

stile

car park

A66

Outdoor Leisure
N-E Sheet

Starting and
Finishing Point

MAP 26

To Penrith

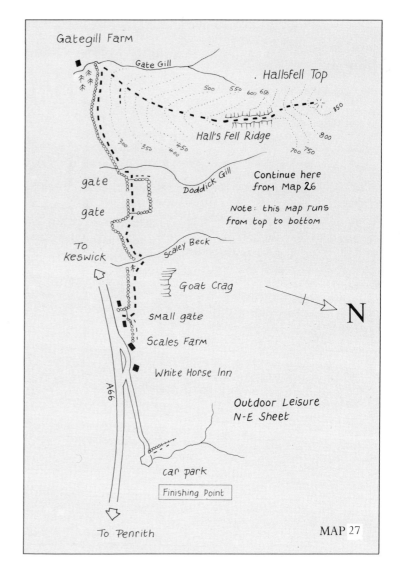

Gategill Farm

Gate Gill

. Hallsfell Top

500 550 600 650

Hall's Fell Ridge

300 350 400 450 700 750 800 850

gate

Doddick Gill

Continue here
from Map 26

gate

Note: this map runs
from top to bottom

To
Keswick

Scaley Beck

Goat Crag

N

small gate

Scales Farm

White Horse Inn

A66

Outdoor Leisure
N-E Sheet

car park

Finishing Point

To Penrith

MAP 27

ROUTE DESCRIPTION (Maps 26, 27)

Walk back along the road, over the stone bridge and look out
for a slate sign in a wall on your R: 'Glenderamackin 1,
Mungrisedale 3'. At this point, turn R, along a track to a farm
gate. Cross via the stile alongside and keep straight ahead,
following the wire fence on your L. Walk along the edge of a
marshy field and the fence becomes a low, hawthorn hedge.
Ahead you can see the footpath winding up a broad, green ridge.
After 100 yards (91 m), the footpath starts to follow the field
boundary around to the left. Stay with it for 10 yards (9 m) until
you come to a gate on your L; the footpath bears off to the R at
this point. Keep following the path which is quite clear as it
strikes out towards the fellside. A fold in the hills turns

The ascent of Sharp Edge

Mousthwaite Comb into a gigantic bowl, open towards the A66, and you are walking around the base of this bowl. The footpath bears R again and begins to ascend the grassy flanks of the ridge between Souther Fell and Scales Fell.

Once at the top of the ridge, turn L towards Scales Fell and you have a good view of Sharp Edge on Blencathra. Follow the ridge and after 400 yards (364 m) you will be joined by a footpath coming in from your L. Below you is an excellent view of River Glenderamackin and the wide, grassy track which runs along the far bank up to the old lead mines.

You follow a fairly eroded path, climbing gradually until you meet up with Scales Beck. Turn L and follow the path uphill, crossing the beck so that the water runs on your L. The path is quite steep and runs through a small gully. After 300 yards (273 m) you climb the rise to arrive at Scales Tarn.

This is a peaceful little tarn, dramatically placed against Tarn Crags and Sharp Edge. The tarn itself is quite shallow and you can see the bottom as it gently shelves away. Sharp Edge is the magnificent arête on your R. It is best to try and arrive at this point fairly early in the day to get up onto the ridge.

Climb the steep path running up to the start of the ridge and then begin to walk out onto the rocks. There are steep drops on either side of you. At the beginning, there is a path which runs 5 feet (1.5 m) below the top of the ridge, on the R—though you still get purists who insist on walking along the absolute apex.

The route can be a scramble in some places. The final stretch of the ridge involves walking past a boulder which seems to lean out over the path; in fact, there is plenty of room to simply walk past and you will only have difficulties if you start to hug too close to the rock. As you reach the end of Sharp Edge you are confronted by the aptly-named Foule Crag. This is a steep, rough scramble before you find yourself on a steeply rolling grass slope and climb to the summit of Blencathra.

Once at the top, all is peace and tranquility after the excitement and tensions of the ascent. Before you is a broad, open moorland plateau. Follow the path as it curves gently round to the summit cairn.

The views from here can be absolutely exhilarating. Look below to Threlkeld and follow the line of the river eastwards until you come to an old railway viaduct *(1)*.

As you face south, the footpath off the summit lies directly in front of you and starts with another steep drop. You come down onto a clearly defined footpath which proceeds down Hall's Fell Ridge. This rocky ridge is quite easy to negotiate, taking a certain amount of care across any loose stone and rubble but can be treacherous in wet or icy conditions. Doddick Gill forms a steep gorge to your L. After just over $\frac{1}{2}$ mile (0.8 km), you start to level off across a heather-covered fellside. Continue down to Gategill Farm, ignoring the path on your L as you get within 200 yards (182 m) of the farm. You approach a stone wall, enclosing a conifer plantation, just behind the farm. Turn L and follow the wall along the foot of the fellside.

The path crosses Doddick Gill and continues along the wall until, almost 1 mile (1.6 km) from Gate Gill, it drops down a shallow gorge to cross Scaley Beck. Once across onto the other bank, resume following the wall until you come to a kissing gate on your R. Go through, between two cottages, and you find yourself beside the A66. Turn L, following the road past Scales Farm to the White Horse Inn, whereupon you bear L onto the minor road which takes you back to the car.

1 Mosedale Viaduct

This was once part of the line that connected Penrith and Cockermouth. When the line opened, in 1865, it put Keswick on the Victorian tourist map. The route eventually fell foul of Beeching's axe, but the section from Threlkeld to Keswick has recently been re-opened as a delightful, low-level footpath. A walk sheet giving map and directions is available from any National Park information centre.

Looking down on Scales Tarn from Foule Crag

2.17

SKIDDAW

STARTING AND FINISHING POINT
Car park above Underscar (NW-282254) north of Keswick.
LENGTH
8½ miles (13.6 km)
ASCENT
2180 ft (660 m)

Skiddaw is a friendly, rounded mountain, not too unkind to those who insist on attempting it in plimsoles or wellies. This route, which follows the broad footpath from Underscar car park, must be one of the easiest ways imaginable to ascend a 3000 ft (900 m) peak. The descent requires a little compass work but then it is a straightforward return route, giving you a glimpse of the splendour and isolation of Mungrisedale.

ROUTE DESCRIPTION (Maps 28, 29)

The tiny, windswept car park above Underscar gives a hint of the views you can expect on this walk; already you are high enough to look out over Bassenthwaite and Thornthwaite Forest. Keswick and Derwent Water, however, are largely obscured by Latrigg. Walk to the end of the car park—the opposite end to the approach road—and at the fence cross a stile and turn L (PFS 'Skiddaw, Bassenthwaite'). A muddy path goes between the boundaries of two fields, crossing a stile half-way, and arrives at a farm gate after 300 yards (273 m). Cross the stile alongside and the path forks two ways. The R-hand fork is more of a track. Bear half-L instead and begin to walk uphill. You are now heading back, parallel with the road, having just walked around three sides of the field on your L. The rounded flanks of Skiddaw rise before you.

Memorial to Edward and Joseph Hawell of Lonscale

   As you start to go uphill, you will pass a stone memorial cross on your R *(1)*. Keep to the track and the climb gets steadily steeper. The path is a broad, eroded scar at this point, so you will only have difficulty following it if there is snow on the ground. Keep to the fence on your L and, after 800 yards (728 m), you will come to a farm gate. The fence does a dogleg at this point, to cross the path. Climb over the stile next to the gate and continue following the fence, this time on your R. As the gradient eases off slightly, look back and you have wonderful views over Derwent Water and Keswick. Keep ascending, following the fence on your R until you come to a small iron gate. Go through and a very obvious track winds before you,

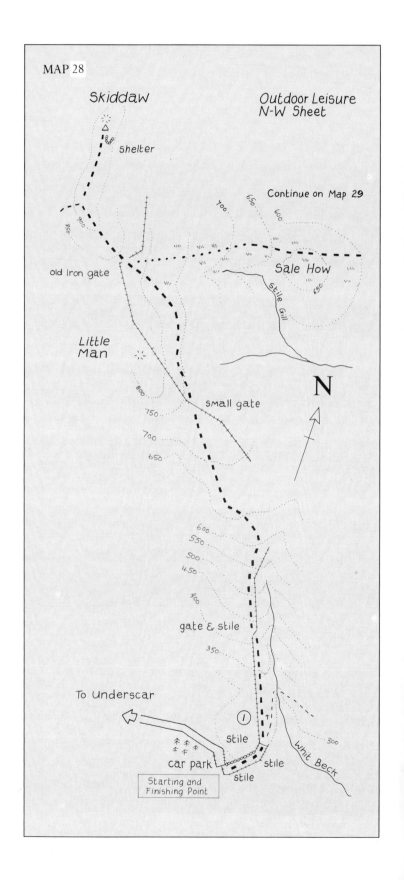

Opposite *Skiddaw from Surprise View*

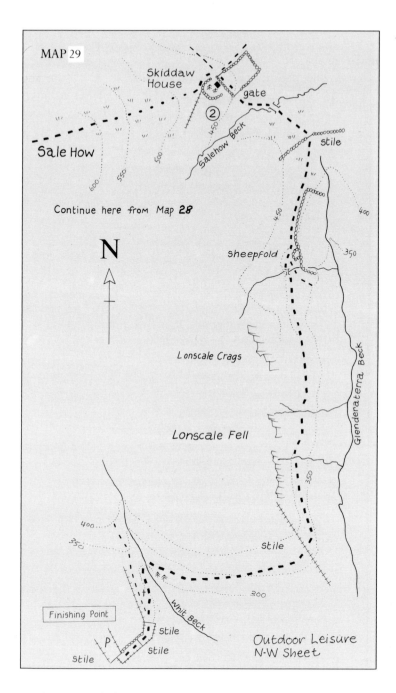

MAP 29

Skiddaw House

gate

Sale How

Salehow Beck

stile

②

450

500

550

600

350

Continue here from Map 28

400

450

N

Sheepfold

Lonscale Crags

350

Glenderaterra Beck

Lonscale Fell

350

stile

400

350

stile

300

Finishing Point

Whit Beck

P

stile

stile

Outdoor Leisure
N·W Sheet

stile

working round the eastern flank of Little Man.

The track remains straightforward and level for perhaps ½ mile (0.8 km) before starting to climb again. You come to a fence—broken in places—and an iron gate. Go through and bear L slightly, making a sharp ascent to the ridge. Follow the ridge to the summit of Skiddaw.

The summit itself is quite crowded; in addition to a stone shelter and an OS obelisk, there is also a stone viewfinder, built in 1977 to commemorate the Queen's Silver Jubilee. Use this finder as a guide to the stupendous 360 degree views.

From the summit, retrace your steps to the iron gate and broken fence. As the path winds away in front of you, stand at the gate and look due east, across a stretch of grassy moorland to Sale How, a small, rounded hill $\frac{3}{4}$ mile (1.2 km) away. There is a distinct track running across the hill, but no apparent footpath between the gate and the start of this track. This, however, is the route to Skiddaw House and our return path. So, leaving the main footpath, head down across the hillside, keeping Sale How directly ahead of you at all times. It remains in view at all times, so there really is no possibility of getting lost.

You hit the start of the track before you reach Sale How. Follow the track over the hill and drop down the other side of Sale How, coming into sight of a wide, river valley and a small, isolated clump of conifers. The track heads directly towards the trees.

One hundred yards (91 m) from the trees, you meet a wire fence and a sheep enclosure on your R. Bear L, along the fence, until you reach the stone wall encircling the trees. Follow the wall L, working round the plantation until you come to Skiddaw House itself (2).

There is a path through the grounds, running in front of the house, but the right-of-way bears L, along the stone wall for a short distance, and then R, to run along the wall in front of the house, keeping the house on your R. Keep to the wall and you walk beyond the house, through a gate and down the track to Salehow Beck. Turn half-L along the beck until you come to a wooden bridge. Cross the bridge and the track meanders across open moorland for 300 yards (273 m) until it arrives at a stone wall. Cross the stile alongside and the footpath bears half-R, away from the wall. Ahead of you is the dramatic, conical shape of Lonscale Fell.

The track starts to climb and runs along an old stone wall on your L. After 400 yards (364 m) you come to a sheepfold, next to the wall on your L, and the path splits two ways. Go half-R and follow the path to a wooden footbridge which spans a tiny, fast-flowing beck. Once over the beck, the path splits again. The path to the R merely cuts a corner, so is only advised if the path below is badly flooded. Go half-L, crossing another beck and continue along the track.

You begin to climb high above Glenderaterra Beck, on your L and find yourself amidst very impressive, rolling fells. The fells of Mungrisedale have an air of wild immensity which comes from sheer size and isolation and has nothing to do with dramatic drops or fierce crags. It is an attractive, little-explored area (but I am not allowed to say more or my walking friends will disown me).

The path levels off below Lonscale Crags. You have now climbed very high above the valley floor and have a good view of the three waterfalls on the opposite fell. Above the line of Blease Fell you can see the cruel ridge of Blencathra.

Continue along the path until you suddenly round the corner of Lonscale fell and Threlkeld and the A66 lies before you (3). Follow the path R, around the grassy flanks of the fell and you come back into sight of Derwent Water.

Almost immediately, you arrive at a wire fence, cutting across in front of you. There are two farm gates and, between them, a wooden stile. Cross and keep following the level grass track. Below you, to the L, you will see an attractive farm, tucked away behind a fold in the hillside. This is Lonscale Farm. Ahead you can see the stone cross and the car park.

Within $\frac{1}{2}$ mile (0.8 km) of the car park, the path suddenly descends into a pretty ravine, with an attractive waterfall. Ford the beck (no proper stepping stones) and bear half-L. Walk uphill, away from this pretty, unexpected spot and the track joins the outgoing path at a farm gate, just below the memorial cross. Retrace your route back to the car park.

1 Memorial cross

This stone cross bears an inscription which reads: 'In loving memory of two Skiddaw shepherds—Edward Hawell of Lonscale, born October 21st, 1815, died June 2nd, 1889, and his son, Joseph Hawell of Lonscale, born December 24th, 1854, died February 20th, 1891. Noted breeders of prize Herdwick sheep.'

2 Skiddaw House

Skiddaw House was built some time during the nineteenth century and was originally the gamekeeper's house, attached to Cockermouth Castle, at a time when Skiddaw forest was extensively used for hunting. It has also, at times, been a shepherd's bothy, and was attached to the Quaker school at Wigton. In June, 1987, it was opened as a Youth Hostel, to provide simple accommodation.

3 A66

One of Lakeland's least attractive features. Built despite fierce opposition from the NPA and the Friends of the Lake District. The then Secretary of State for the Department of the Environment, Geoffrey Rippon, overruled the wishes of the local planning authority and, in 1973, gave the go-ahead for work to proceed. The A66 now roars its way along the western shores of Bassenthwaite Lake to Cockermouth.

View towards Sale How and the return route

3.18

SCAFELL PIKE

STARTING AND FINISHING POINT
The road approaching Seathwaite Farm, Borrowdale (NW-235122). Do not park or turn round in the farmyard—the farmer will get cross—but there is ample space for parking on the verge of the road. If no luck, use the car park in Seatoller and walk back.

LENGTH
8½ miles (13.5 km)

ASCENT
3160 ft (958 m)

Scafell Pike is 3210 feet (978 m) high, which makes it the highest point in England and an irresistable magnet, drawing even the most indifferent fellwalker to its summit. Its great popularity means that it has one of the highest accident rates of the Lakeland fells; a result of the sheer numbers who climb the mountain, rather than any inherent dangers. Abrupt changes in weather conditions or sudden mist can make it a difficult and confusing peak for the ill-prepared.

There are many routes to the summit, but this is one of the best. It takes in a number of subsidiary peaks and brings you, after a long day's walk, back via the exhilarating spectacle of Taylor Gill Force.

Summit cairn on Scafell Pike—the highest point in England

Scafell from Scafell Pike

ROUTE DESCRIPTION (Maps 30, 31)

Walk along the road towards Seathwaite Farm *(1)*, the fells rising steeply on either side of you. To your R is Sourmilk Gill— not to be confused with Sourmilk Gill in Easedale. Walk straight into the farmyard, passing the farmhouse and (in summer) a small cafe on your L. Note well the archway in the barn on your R; you will be returning through here. Continue along a rough farm track and 80 yards (73 m) beyond the farm buildings you will come to a footpath on your L to Borrowdale via Thorneythwaite. Disregarding the path, continue straight ahead, through a farmgate and bearing around to the L of a small group of conifers. You pass through another farm gate as you draw alongside the conifers.

Once past the trees, you are walking across an open valley floor, strewn with rocks and boulders. You can see the path winding up the fellside ahead of you.

You cross a small wooden footbridge and continue along the track to another farm gate. Go through and straight on. So far, you have gained hardly any height. You approach a pretty packhorse bridge *(2)* and cross to the R-hand bank of Grains Gill where you are confronted by a stone wall and yet another farm gate. Once through, there is a junction in the path. Turn L and follow the line of the wall. After 100 yards (91 m), pass through a much-broken stone wall; the track has shrunk to a narrow footpath which is climbing quite steadily above the level of the gill on your L. The path climbs to a narrow gate and goes beyond to bring you to a wooden bridge—White Bridge— which crosses the gill.

There now follows a long stretch of well-maintained footpath (courtesy of the National Trust). Look out for some nice pools in the beck on your R. As you approach the buttress of Great End, the stream plunges through a dramatic gorge. This has a wild, unexplored look and is a good place to look for some unusual species of plant which have escaped the ravages of the sheep. (Whether they also escape the ravages of the gill scramblers is another matter.)

The footpath levels out and to your R is a good view of the reddish scree of Hell Gill, on Great Gable. Carry straight on, towards the towering cliff of Broad Crag and once you have crossed the beck, turn L and follow the stream. As you skirt round the base of Great End, ignore the path to your L and keep to the R. The path climbs and as it levels out once more you arrive at a large stone cairn on Esk Hause. Ahead of you is Esk

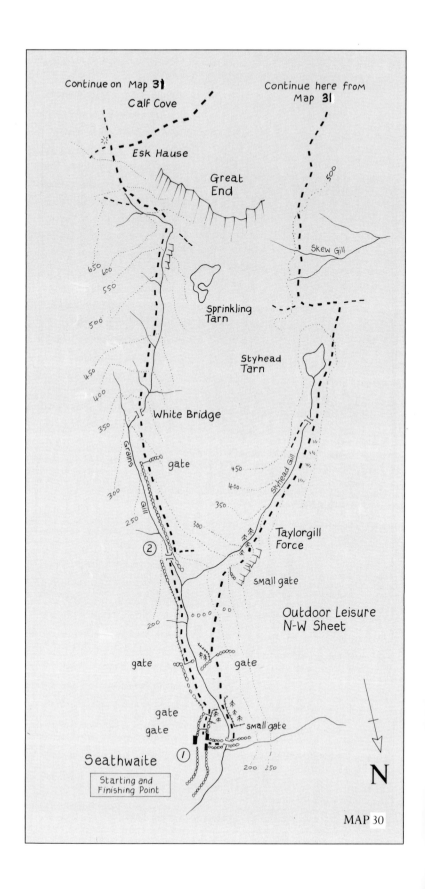

Pike and a good view of the Langdales. Here you find yourself at a junction of several footpaths. Go R, marked by cairns, and continue along a broad scar in the fellside, walking into the boulder-strewn area of Calf Cove.

The track is easy to follow if you keep to an eroded streak across the boulders and levels out once more above the cove. If you walk off the path a short distance at this point, onto a rocky promontory, you have a good view of the head of Wasdale. Back to the path and begin to bear L, up the boulder slopes of Broad Crag. It is $\frac{1}{2}$ mile (0.8 km) of rough level walking to the summit, dropping to a saddle before beginning the final ascent to Scafell Pike.

You follow a sharp, boulder-strewn path up onto the ridge which is once again very rough and steep. Finally, you arrive at the summit cairn (3). You are now at the highest point in England.

From the summit, head north-west, past the OS obelisk, and you can see a path running ahead of you. Keep to the line of

Mountain rescue box at Styhead Tarn

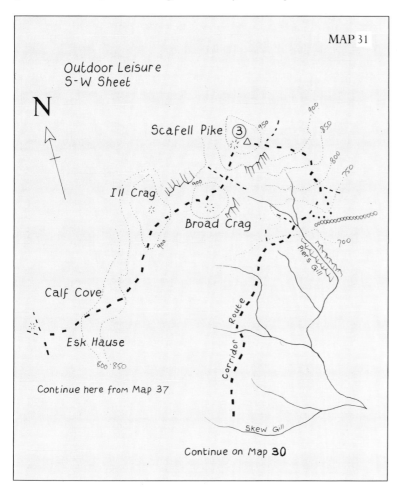

115

cairns and after 100 yards (91 m), where the footpath divides, bear R. After a steep descent, the gradient eases off and you walk onto a fellside covered in grass—a great relief after the boulders. The path splits again. Go straight down to join a stone wall and a good view of Wasdale, then follow the wall R (without crossing it) until you hit a rocky band coming down from your R and you can then see a path ahead of you which climbs up to rejoin the main track. At the track, bear L and follow it around the base of Broad Crag.

You arrive at Piers Gill, a fierce gorge which plummets down between Lingmell and Great End, towards Wasdale. Cross the head of the gorge and bear L, continuing downhill past a pair of boggy tarns (i.e. do not follow the gorge down). The route leads you to a rock face. Climb alongside the crag (do not go beyond the broken stone wall) and you come up onto the top of Stand Crag, with a view down to Lingmell.

There follows a steep descent to Spout Head and a badly-eroded gully. At a T-junction in the path, go L, following the main track and skirt down to a mountain rescue box. At the box, turn R and walk down to the tarn.

The path follows Styhead Gill downstream and, 500 yards (455 m) below the tarn, you come to a wooden footbridge. The main bridleway crosses the beck at this point but a much more picturesque route is to keep to the L-hand bank and follow the beck downstream to Taylorgill Force. This 90 ft (27 m) cascade is considered by many to be the most spectacular in the Lake District, more for its setting than the actual height of the fall. It stands amidst a small group of conifers and looks out over wild crags to the head of Seathwaite. A short detour to stand beside the head of the cascade is essential.

Walk past the falls onto a narrow path which follows a vertiginous route beneath a steep crag. As you work your way out onto the path you have an increasingly good view of the waterfall. After a very careful 200 yards (182 m), you come to a small gate. Go through, down six stone steps and continue to pick your way downhill.

The path passes through an old stone wall and begins to level out, staying above, but parallel to, the gill. Cross another stone wall via a ladder stile and in the distance you can see a small conifer plantation and Seathwaite Farm. A clear path through bracken lies ahead of you. Continue downhill, past a plantation on your L until you come to the river, passing through a wooden gate to arrive at a footbridge. Cross the river and follow the broad track in front of you, between two stone walls. This brings you back through the archway between the barns. Turn L and retrace your route to the car.

Grains Gill above Stockley Bridge

1 *Seathwaite*

Seathwaite is renowned for having the highest rainfall in England. The actual basis for this is apocryphal, but it does average around 130 in (330 cm) a year. It is not that it rains more often here, just that it rains harder. By comparison, at Keswick, only 8 miles (13 km) away, the rainfall averages only 51 in (130 cm) a year. For the record, Sprinkling Tarn has the highest rainfall; an average of 185 in (470 cm) a year.

2 *Stockley Bridge*

One consequence of the heavy rainfall in this part of the world is the mass of rocks and boulders which lie across the valley floor, washed down by the beck. In August 1966, there was a tremendous storm and in the heavy flooding that followed, the old packhorse bridge was largely destroyed and had to be rebuilt.

3 *Summit Cairn*

The summit cairn on Scafell Pike, built in 1921, bears a plaque which commemorates the men of the Lake District who 'fell for God and King, for freedom, peace and right in the Great War 1914–18'.

THE MANIFOLD VALLEY

STARTING AND FINISHING
POINT
Car-park at Wetton Mill near
Butterton (119-095561).
LENGTH
5½ miles (9 km)
ASCENT
900 ft (280 m)

The Manifold Valley has, like its more famous sister Dovedale, limestone caverns and cliffs. However, as well as being usually much quieter it also has a disappearing river, Thor's Cave, which is in fact bigger than any in Dovedale and a veritable honeycomb of disused shafts and levels in the copper mines of Ecton Hill.

ROUTE DESCRIPTION (Map 32)

From the car-park, go over the bridge and L up the road to Dale Farm. Go through the farmyard to the L of the farmhouse, under the pipes ('Headroom 5 ft 8 in') and through the gate to walk up the dale. Continue until you come immediately below the Sugarloaf, a steep, limestone reef knoll, and skirt it to the L on a small path which climbs to a PFS. Go over the stile and then the one immediately to its L. Follow the fence and then the wall and, after crossing one more stile, reach a farm road ½ mile (800 m) beyond the Sugarloaf. Turn immediately L through the gate and, heading for Summerhill Farm, follow the R wall up to the next gate. Cross the field diagonally, passing an old lime kiln on the L, and go through a passage between walls into the next field. Cross this, again diagonally, to a similar passage, and turn half L to follow the wall through a gap and over a stile to turn R on a clear path a few yards down the hillside. In the valley below is Swainsley Hall, built in 1867 by a London solicitor, with a dovecote in its grounds. The Manifold Railway ran through a tunnel behind the hall, to conceal it from the owners.

The path stays level and then sweeps round the great bowl-shaped hillside above the Ecton Copper Mines *(1)*, gradually dropping to the spoil heaps of the Dutchman Mine. Ahead is the engine house of Deep Ecton Mine and here the path doubles back along the ridge beside the wall, passing fenced, open mineshafts to a stile. The path continues on the L-hand side of the ridge, passing more shafts and levels, through two wall gaps and over three stiles to the ruined buildings of Waterbank Mine. From the mine, the road is reached after 300 yards (270 m) at a

Wetton Mill on the River Manifold

gate. Turn L down the road and, ignoring the L turning, continue through the gate and down the road for ½ mile (800 m) to Pepper Inn, now a private house, but once used as an isolation hospital when there was an outbreak of smallpox among navvies building the Manifold Light Railway.

A stile opposite leads to a small bridge over the stream, and then a wall on the R is followed up to a stile in the corner over the fence. Cross the field half L to the next stile and straight ahead over the brow of the hill to a stile with a quarry on the R. Crossing the stile ahead, go through the gate opposite and down the farm lane to the village of Wetton. Turn R and walk through the village to the far end. Turn R at the T-junction and then L at the fork (sign 'Concession Footpath'). In just under ½ mile (800 m) go through a gate and over the stile to the R (PFS). Go L down to the gap in the ruined wall at the corner, across the dip and up to a stile. A short steep climb leads to the summit of the cliffs above Thor's Cave. Be very careful; the cliff edge is unprotected and quite sheer.

Return the same way and turn L to circle down to the base of the cliffs at the entrance to Thor's Cave *(2)*. Once this huge natural cavern has been explored, a flight of stone steps will lead you down to the River Manifold. The river is usually dry, but is crossed by a substantial bridge. Turn R on the old track of the Manifold Light Railway *(3)* and in ½ mile (800 m), crossing another bridge, turn L to follow either of two parallel roads back to the car-park at Wetton Mill *(4)*.

1 Ecton Copper Mines
In the eighteenth century, Deep Ecton Mine was a very profitable mine for its owner the Duke of Devonshire, with

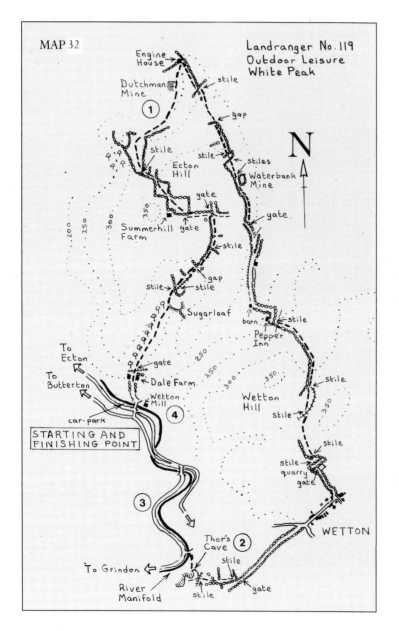

MAP 32

Landranger No. 119
Outdoor Leisure
White Peak

Engine House

Dutchman Mine

①

stile

gap

stile · stile · stiles

Ecton Hill

Waterbank Mine

N

gate

350 · 300 · 250 · 200

Summerhill gate
Farm

gate

stile

gap

stile → ← stile

Sugarloaf

barn · stile

Pepper Inn

To Ecton

To Butterton

gate

← Dale Farm.

Wetton Hill

250 · 250 · 300 · 350 · 350

stile

Wetton Hill

car-park

④

stile

STARTING AND
FINISHING POINT

stile

stile
quarry
gate

③

WETTON

Thor's Cave ②

stile

To Grindon ←

stile

gate

River Manifold

profits amounting to over one million pounds. It was, at 1380 ft (420 m), the deepest mine in Great Britain.

Deep Ecton Mine was just one of a number of copper mines to be found at Ecton, all of which are now disused and in ruins. The Ecton copper mines also saw in 1670 the earliest use in Britain of gunpowder in mining and at its peak around 300 men, women and children worked here. Sixty men worked a six-hour shift for about 5p, while boys removed the ore to be crushed above ground by women and girls.

Near Alstonefield

Although the Ecton copper mines did not suffer the serious water problems often found elsewhere in the Peak, a 32 ft diameter (10 m) waterwheel was built underground to power drainage pumps and boats were used as transport some 200 ft (60 m) beneath the River Manifold. The engine house, still in use as a barn, held a Boulton and Watt engine which raised waste rock to the surface, forming great spoil heaps since removed for road making. The mines finally ceased production in the late nineteenth century.

2 *Thor's Cave*

Thor's Cave, the cave of the Norse Thunder God, looks down on the Manifold Valley from a very large main entrance, 30 ft (9 m) high and over 20 ft (6 m) wide. A second side entrance, West Window, faces down the valley. First excavated by Samuel Carrington from Wetton in 1864, the cave has yielded stone querns, pottery fragments, bronze brooches, iron knives and bones from Romano-British times. Much has probably been lost by the early excavators who made a large spoil heap outside the cave entrance. The pieces of tape seen hanging from high in the roof are left by rock climbers whose spectacular climb 'Thor' goes up the wall, crosses the roof and then ascends the cliff.

3 *Manifold Light Railway*

Opened in 1904 and closed again by 1934, this railway fell between the heyday of steam and the modern preservation societies who would surely have rescued it. It took two years to build and was said by a navvy to 'start from nowhere and end up in the same place'. A private, narrow gauge railway of 2 ft 6 in (762 mm), it operated mainly as a milk train, supplementing meagre passenger traffic with excursion trains at weekends and public holidays. There was a connecting milk train from the main line at Waterhouses from 1919 and 300 churns a day were carried. When the dairy closed in 1933 the railway rapidly succumbed, being converted to a footpath in 1937.

4 *Wetton Mill*

Wetton Mill, now a farm, but originally a corn mill, was first mentioned in records of 1577. The bridge is much later, dating from 1807. Just above the bridge at Wetton Mill is a limestone hummock, full of interesting holes, known as Nan Tor Cave. The River Manifold disappears just below the mill and travels 5 miles (8 km) underground before reappearing at the 'Boil Hole' in the grounds of Ilam Hall. Sir Thomas Wardle of Swainsley Hall unsuccessfully attempted to block the swallow holes with concrete, but the river won and only sometimes, usually in winter, appears above ground.

1.20

Edensor and Chatsworth Park

STARTING AND FINISHING
POINT
Calton Lees car-park just off B6012,
Beeley–Baslow road (119-259684).
LENGTH
4 miles (6.5 km)
ASCENT
400 ft (120 m)

Although this walk follows public rights-of-way, a large part of the Chatsworth Estate is in fact freely open to the public to wander at will by the courtesy of the Duke and Duchess of Devonshire. Edensor village is a most charming place, while a visit to Chatsworth itself would complete a very pleasant day out.

ROUTE DESCRIPTION (Map 33)

From the car-park beside the B6012 walk towards the garden centre, through a gate ('No Thro' Road'), and follow the road

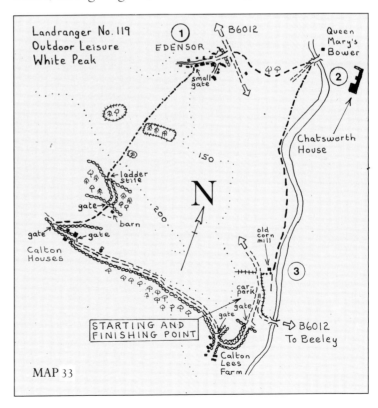

round the bend to the track junction by Calton Lees Farm. Go straight across through the gate and follow the track for ¾ mile (1·2 km) to Calton Houses. The track goes through a gate, between buildings, and out into the field at a gate. Turn R and the path leads across the field and into the wood at a gate to the L of a barn. To the R is Russian Cottage, named from the friendship between the sixth Duke of Devonshire and the Czar.

Emerging over a ladder stile into Chatsworth Park, aim just L of the spire of Edensor Church and cross the parkland. Enter Edensor *(1)* at a small gate and some steps by the church, and turn R past the fine stone cottages. Cross the B6012 to the gravel path opposite which climbs through a stand of beech trees with a good view of Chatsworth *(2)* ahead. Descend to the bridge and turn R to follow the river for a mile (1·6 km) to the old corn mill *(3)*. Climb up the bank and cross the road to the car-park.

1 Edensor

Pronounced 'Ensor', the present village is of very recent origin. In 1755 the views from Chatsworth were improved by the demolition of all that could be seen of the old village. In 1839 the rest of the village, although hidden in the valley bottom, was also demolished with the single exception of a cottage which still stands today isolated on the other side of the road. The new village was designed by Sir Joseph Paxton (of Crystal Palace fame), and the church of St Peter, consecrated in 1866, was the work of Sir Gilbert Scott. The past Dukes of Devonshire and their families lie in a quiet corner of the churchyard, but visitors come here to visit another grave, that of Kathleen Kennedy, daughter of Joseph Kennedy, United States Ambassador to Britain and sister of the late John Kennedy, President of the United States, whose visit on 29 June 1963 is commemorated on a plaque in front of the grave.

2 Chatsworth

This magnificent mansion is principally the creation of the first Duke of Devonshire who between 1686 and 1707 practically rebuilt the original house piecemeal and also built the great cascade in the grounds.

The first house on this site was built in 1552 by Sir William Cavendish and his celebrated wife, Bess of Hardwick. The house faced east and the Cavendish Hunting Tower, which dates from this time, remains in its splendid position on the hillside above the house. Queen Mary's Bower, a kind of

Chatsworth House

Edensor churchyard

summer house near the bridge and dating from the same time, encloses an ancient earthwork and was frequented by Mary Queen of Scots when she was a prisoner at Chatsworth in the custody of the Earl of Shrewsbury, Bess of Hardwick's fourth husband. Mary was here on five occasions between 1570 and 1581.

In the time of the fourth Duke the grounds were extensively remodelled under the direction of Capability Brown, and new roads, which ran north–south, replaced the former east–west alignment. The sixth Duke added the famous Emperor Fountain which throws a jet of water 290 ft (90 m) into the air, which when built was the second highest fountain in the world.

The house itself contains a splendid collection of treasures, paintings, tapestries, sculptures and other works of art, and in the grounds there are large herds of fallow deer.

3 *Old Corn Mill*

This mill, built about 1760 in a style complementary to Chatsworth House, was in operation, grinding corn, until 1950. A millstone still leans against an outer wall. During a gale in 1962 the building was badly damaged when trees fell on it, and now only the shell remains by the side of the River Derwent.

1.21

THREE SHIRE HEADS

STARTING AND FINISHING
POINT
Lay-by on A54 Congleton–Buxton
road near Danebower Quarries
(119-008699).
LENGTH
4½ miles (7 km) or 3 miles (5 km)
variant
ASCENT
700 ft (215 m)

The gritstone packhorse bridge at Three Shire Heads, where the counties of Derbyshire, Cheshire and Staffordshire meet, is not far from the road, but in a short walk you can feel very far away from the rush of the present day as you look down on Panniers Pool and think of the packhorse trains moving slowly through this countryside. In fact you are in the middle of a once industrial area which only recently has reverted to the wild state seen today.

The walk crosses the infant River Dane which in exceptionally wet weather can be difficult; if so, go out and back to Three Shire Heads by the return route.

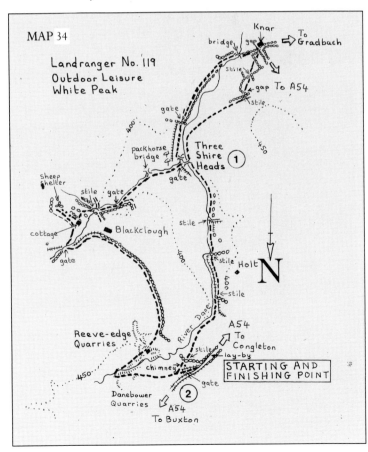

ROUTE DESCRIPTION (Map 34)

A few yards from the lay-by, towards Buxton, take the track towards a chimney which is all that remains of the Dane Colliery. Go through a gate and follow the track through Danebower Quarries to the River Dane. Cross the river, turn R and follow the track up to Reeve-edge Quarries and continue beside the wall.

The view gradually opens out as the track veers L away from the River Dane. The moorland on the R, pitted with depressions, speaks of the industrial past of this area when coal was dug from many small mines. Shortly you come to Blackclough Farm on the R and then the path rounds the head of a clough, crossing an iron gate.

As the main track bends L immediately above a small cottage, leave it and take a descending minor track which leads in roughly the same direction. Just before an unusual T-shaped sheep shelter, the right-of-way doubles back. Aim for the cottage, turn L through the gateposts, and head directly downhill to pass through a tumbledown wall. At the field corner the path meets the road by the entrance to Blackclough Farm. Turn R and take the R fork following the stream. Go through an iron gate and very shortly take the L fork continuing to follow the stream downhill, passing an interesting small packhorse bridge on the L, to reach Three Shire Heads *(1)* at a gate. The shorter variant now turns R over the bridge.

For the longer route do not cross the packhorse bridge ahead, but turn L and take the broad, sandy track which leads across another small bridge. Panniers Pool is the pool immediately below the bridges. In about 200 yards (180 m) pass through an iron gate and take the R fork along the wall. Follow the river until you come to a stout wooden bridge. Cross the bridge and climb up a steep track until Knar Farm is reached at a gate. Do not go through the gate, but turn immediately R onto a grassy track across the field. Go between gateposts at the next wall and then bear L up the hillside to a squeezer stile in the wall above. Turn R and follow the track rising gradually across the hillside through the next field and a small field beyond to emerge over a wooden stile onto a major track. Turn R and after a few yards a sandy track comes in from the L. This track leads gently downhill back to Three Shire Heads where the shorter route is rejoined.

Follow the River Dane upstream and at a five barred gate cross the stile on the R to stay by the river. Where the river

Reeve-edge Quarries

turns R, cross a stile and the field below Holt Farm. As the river meanders back, follow the fence until it meets the wall, where a stile allows you to rejoin the river-bank. A little further on, the ruins of a mine building herald the Dane Colliery (2) which would go unnoticed if it were not for the chimney. The track now leads uphill and over a stile, with the chimney straight ahead. Go through the gate above to rejoin the path back to the main road.

1 Three Shire Heads

At this charming spot by Panniers Pool, four packhorse ways meet to cross the River Dane. The bridge, if examined underneath, will be seen to have been widened on the upstream side, indicating the importance of the crossing and the heavy traffic it must once have seen. A map of 1610 calls this Three Shire Stones.

Packhorse trains, that is strings of up to forty or even fifty horses, were the principal means used for the transport of goods from the Middle Ages until the seventeenth century. Because packhorses could travel over the moors so much more easily than waggons, packhorses were being used in the Peak District well into the nineteenth century. Over boggy ground these tracks were paved with gritstone slabs which often can still be seen. It was, of course, much cheaper to maintain a narrow packhorse track than one for waggons, and bridges could be made narrower too. The name jagger, which occurs in some placenames such as Jaggers Clough on Kinder, was applied to the leader of a packhorse train and comes from Jaeger-galloway, the breed of horse most in use in the Peak District. The packhorses carried many varied loads, one of the earliest being salt, hence the name saltways.

The nearby village of Flash, which at 1518 ft (460 m) above sea level is claimed to be the highest village in England, depended on trade via the packhorse routes as the land hereabouts is poor. However, the ease with which one could escape the law by crossing into an adjacent county at Three Shire Heads led to a certain notoriety for Flash, and its name was applied to the coining of 'flash', or counterfeit, money by the inhabitants.

2 Dane Colliery

The coal mines in the Buxton area were never on the scale of those in the main industrial areas, but before rail transport brought in cheap coal from outside, these mines were important to the local community. Mining started at the beginning of the seventeenth century and continued until as late as World War I, although the principal activity occurred

Knar

in the period 1780 to 1880. The coal was used to burn limestone for use in mortar for building, and also in agriculture for improving the land.

The Blackclough Mine connected underground with the Dane Colliery. Dane Colliery produced some of the best and cleanest coal in the area; the coal of many other mines contained impurities such as sulphur and iron pyrites. The chimney, which is all that remains visible today, was connected by a flue running down the hillside to what was probably an engine house. The remains of the flue can still be seen in places. An opening near the river was the end of the sough or drainage level for the mine.

MONSAL DALE AND ASHFORD IN THE WATER

STARTING AND FINISHING
POINT
White Lodge car-park (119-170705).
On the A6 Buxton–Bakewell road, 3
miles (5 km) west of Bakewell.
LENGTH
8½ miles (13.5 km)
ASCENT
800 ft (240 m)

The lower reaches of the River Wye pass through Monsal Dale, spanned by the great viaduct of the old Buxton to Derby railway, and on down past the village of Ashford in the Water, which is famed for its well dressing, to the town of Bakewell.

Packhorse bridges and old mills blend into the scene, complementing the natural beauty of the dale; while the railway itself becomes in summer a wild flower garden which links with the Wye to form a varied and interesting walk.

ROUTE DESCRIPTION (Maps 35–37)

Cross the A6 to a stile in the wall opposite. Descend to a small stream and over a wooden ladder stile, where in summer the banks of the stream are covered in the bright yellow flowers of musk. Through the woodland beyond (PFS 'Monsal Dale') the first view of the River Wye is seen. On the opposite bank is Fin Cop, whose top is the site of an Iron Age hill fort.

Follow the river upstream for 1¼ miles (2 km) to a stile and under Monsal Viaduct (1). At the footbridge over the river, turn half L through the stile (PFS 'Brushfield and Taddington Dale') and ascend to the disused railway. Go over the stile (sign 'Monsal Trail') to join the railway where the blocked up entrance of a lead mine can be seen opposite. Turn L towards the tunnel to emerge suddenly on the very exposed heights of Monsal Viaduct. Just before the tunnel turn L and after 100 yards (90 m) turn R onto another track. Continue to climb until a flight of stone steps brings you out, somewhat breathless, to Monsal Head (café, pub and toilets).

Cross the B6465 and take the road opposite (an old turnpike) to Little Longstone. Passing the Congregational Church, enter the village and go past (or through!) the Packhorse Inn to turn R over a stone step stile (PFS 'Ashford 1½ ml) just past the last house on the R. Bear half R across four fields to rejoin the tracks of the disused railway.

Opposite Sheepwash Bridge, Ashford in the Water

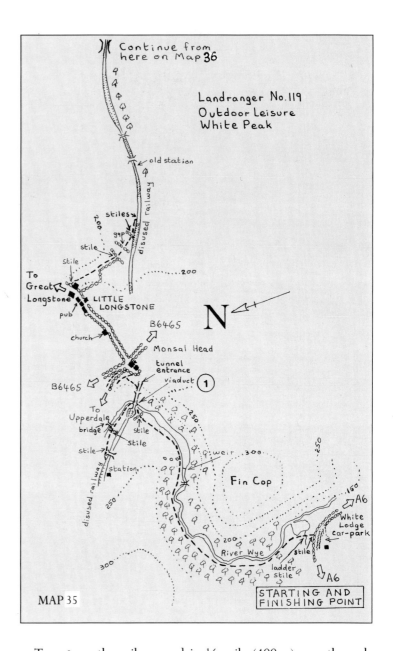

Continue from here on Map **36**

Landranger No. 119
Outdoor Leisure
White Peak

old station

stiles

stile

stile

200

To Great Longstone

LITTLE LONGSTONE

pub

N

church

B6465

Monsal Head

tunnel entrance

B6465

viaduct

①

To Upperdale

bridge

stile

stile

stile

weir 300

station

250

Fin Cop

150

A6

White Lodge car-park

disused railway

250

River Wye

stile

ladder stile

A6

300

200

MAP 35

STARTING AND FINISHING POINT

Turn L on the railway and in ¼ mile (400 m) pass through the old station at Thornbridge Hall. Soon the view to the L opens out with Longstone Edge forming the skyline in the distance. One mile (1.6 km) beyond the station, opposite the Rowdale toll-bar house, with the bell and gate symbol on its gable, take the footpath turning R through a wooden gate (PFS 'Bakewell'). Follow the green path, enclosed by stone walls, over the hill through seven gates to a track to the road.

Go straight ahead to cross Holme Bridge *(2)* and then R onto the A6. Just after the factory, turn R through a stile. Cross the field and go through a narrow path between the houses crossing

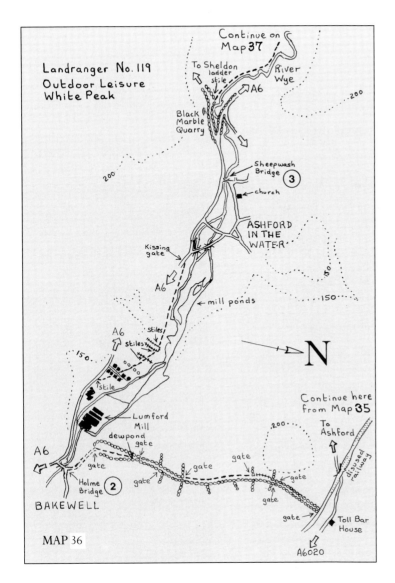

Landranger No. 119
Outdoor Leisure
White Peak

Continue on Map 37

To Sheldon ladder stile

River Wye

Black Marble Quarry

200

200

Sheepwash Bridge ③

church

ASHFORD IN THE WATER

A6

Kissing gate

mill ponds

150

A6

stiles

stiles

N

Continue here from Map 35

200

To Ashford

stile

Lumford Mill

dewpond gate

gate

gate

gate

gate

gate

gate

Holme Bridge ②

BAKEWELL

MAP 36

Toll Bar House

A6020

disused railway

a road to emerge again into open fields. Follow the meadows to Ashford, over three stiles and passing the millponds, to emerge onto the A6 at a kissing gate. Turn R to cross the two bridges (the second dated 1664). Over the road, enter Ashford in the Water *(3)* and turn L by the village store to pass the Church of the Holy Trinity. At the end where the street turns R, Sheepwash Bridge will be seen on the L. Turn L over the bridge to the A6. Cross this and turn R to gain the relative safety of the footpath on the far side. After about 300 yards (260 m) take the minor road (PFS 'Monsal Dale avoiding A6 road'), passing on the L the Ashford Black Marble Quarry (worked until 1905). Two hundred yards (180 m) along this road, just past a recently restored bridge on the site of the Black Marble Mill, turn R (PFS 'Monsal Dale via White Lodge') and over a ladder stile.

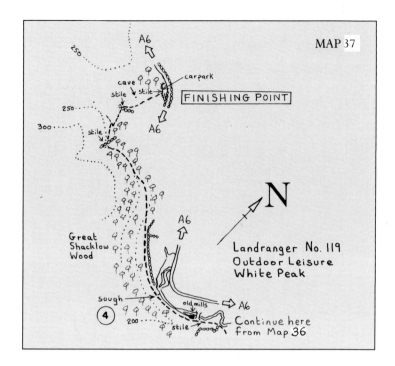

Follow the fields beside the river for ½ mile (800 m) to a stile and the remains of old mills, one of which used to pump drinking water up to Sheldon. Go behind the mills into Great Shacklow Wood and in 200 yards (180 m) the sough of Magpie Mine *(4)* will be seen entering the river on the R. The path now climbs up the hillside and in ⅔ mile (1.1 km) descends to a stile. Continue to the lowest point of the path and turn R (PBS 'Bridleway to A6'). Cross the stile, turn R, and shortly before arriving back at the car-park there is, hidden in the trees above, Taddington Dale Resurgence Cave from which a stream issues in wet weather.

1 Monsal Viaduct

Monsal Viaduct is a most spectacular feature. Built in 1867, the Midland railway ran here until it was closed in 1968, and now the viaduct has been declared of architectural and historic interest. John Ruskin, the nineteenth-century English author and art critic, was less enthusiastic about the railway, declaring 'You enterprised a railroad through the valley – you blasted its rocks away, heaped thousands of tons of shale into its lovely stream. The valley is gone and the Gods with it, and now every fool in Buxton can be at Bakewell in half an hour and every fool in Bakewell at Buxton; which you think a lucrative process of exchange – you Fools everywhere.'

Monsal Dale and the viaduct from Monsal Head

If the weather is unkind it is worth knowing that by turning R instead of L on joining the railway, one of the old buildings of the Monsal Dale railway station will be found still standing.

2 *Holme Bridge*

This was rebuilt in 1664 on a packhorse route to the north. The bridge was probably built at this point in order to avoid payment of tolls at Bakewell itself. A corn mill at Bakewell, recorded as far back as the *Domesday Book*, was supplied with water from this river. When, in 1778, Lumford Mill was built by Richard Arkwright and a reservoir was constructed for the new mill, a bypass leat was built to feed the old mill; this however was not entirely adequate for the purpose, to the annoyance of its owner the Duke of Rutland. In 1852, with the addition of two larger waterwheels to Lumford Mill, another reservoir was constructed upstream, as well as a new channel; while a weir was built in the river to improve the supply to the corn mill.

3 *Ashford in the Water*

Ashford in the Water is one of the villages which continues the ancient tradition of well dressing. About 150 years ago the present floral patterns were introduced. Petals, berries, bark and suchlike are pressed into a bed of clay to form beautiful pictures and patterns. As many as five wells are dressed in Ashford for Trinity Sunday and can be seen for the following week.

Sheepwash Bridge is a medieval packhorse bridge; 'sheepwash' refers to the practice of washing sheep by driving them into the river and making them swim across to emerge on the other side.

The name Ashford comes from the Saxon 'Aescforda', where the Old Portway forded the river, and is mentioned in the *Domesday Book* with a reference to 'plumbariae' or places where lead was smelted.

4 *Magpie Mine Sough*

The sough, or drainage tunnel, drains the Magpie Mine. The scree above the entrance indicates the site of the massive explosion which tore this hillside apart and partially blocked the river on 23 April 1966. Water had built up behind a blockage in the mine and eventually burst forth, fortunately without injuring anyone. The Magpie Mine was being worked for lead as early as 1795 and probably earlier than that. The Peak District Mines Historical Society use the main buildings at Sheldon as a Field Centre. The Magpie sough, driven in 1873, and large enough to be navigable by boat, was probably one of the last major soughs dug in this area.

2.23

Ringing Roger and Grindslow Knoll

STARTING AND FINISHING
POINT
Edale car-park (110-124853).
LENGTH
6 miles (9 km)
ASCENT
1200 ft (375 m)

This popular walk from Edale encircles the Grindsbrook Valley keeping close to the edge of the Kinder plateau. There is the feel of the mountains about this walk with the steep drop into the valley always at your side. After a strenuous ascent, Ringing Roger is reached, and, from the summit rocks round to Grindslow Knoll, walkers can be seen far below on their way up Grindsbrook Clough at the start of their long journey north on the Pennine Way.

Route Description (Map 38)

From the car-park turn R under the railway bridge and up into Edale village *(1)* to the Old Nag's Head. Follow the signs for the Pennine Way *(2)* up the unsurfaced track to the iron gates. A

Nether Tor

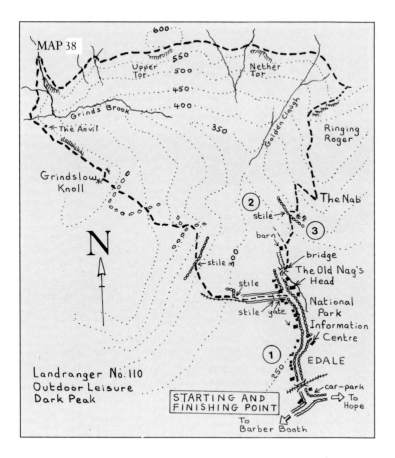

PWS points R on a path which leads down some steps to a bridge. Go along the footpath a short way to a small barn and then turn R and follow the clear path up the field to a stile by Fred Heardman's Plantation *(3)*. The path zig-zags up the hillside to The Nab, which is a good viewpoint for the Vale of Edale spread out below. Contour round towards Golden Clough until you reach the spot immediately below Ringing Roger, and then strike up the hillside directly to the rocks. From the summit, head towards an area of bare rock and sand, and then turn L onto the path which keeps to the edge of the plateau. Crossing Golden Clough, the rocks of Nether Tor on the L are where the stone for Edale Church was quarried.

The path continues along the edge passing the highest point at Upper Tor where Pym Chair can be seen on the distant skyline to the west. Continue to the head of Grindsbrook Clough where it is necessary to turn R and detour for 200 yards (180 m) to avoid the great ravine. Double back on the far side and follow the path round towards Grindslow Knoll, passing the Anvil Stone. The summit of Grindslow Knoll, in just over ¼

Golden Clough

Ringing Roger

mile (400 m), can be missed as the path does not cross the highest point which is a few yards off to the R.

Descend now south-east towards Edale far below. Soon the eroded path improves to a track which leads down to a stile and fields beyond. Cross the field towards a fence and then cross a wall at a stile. A sunken path between hedges is joined, which soon arrives at a stile and a kissing gate opposite the Old Nag's Head. Turn R and walk back down the road to the car-park.

1 *Edale Village*

The village of Edale, the island valley, has two pubs, both of which at one time came under the jurisdiction of Fred Heardman (see *(3)*). There is also a café, an excellent Peak Park Information Centre and several campsites. Despite Edale's popularity, it has not been spoilt and manages to retain much of its charm. Five packhorse ways converged here and there is a good example of a narrow packhorse bridge crossing Grinds Brook only yards from the Old Nag's Head.

2 *The Pennine Way*

Britain's first and most celebrated long-distance footpath stretches 250 miles (400 km) from Edale in the south to Kirk Yetholm over the border in Scotland. This high level route, which follows the Pennine backbone of England, was conceived by Tom Stephenson in 1935; but it took thirty years of dedicated and persistent negotiation before it was finally opened on 24 April 1965. As many as 10000 people a year start on the route, and, although not all of these complete the walk (it is a tough undertaking), its popularity has led to erosion problems such as the four-lane highway up Grindsbrook Clough.

3 *Fred Heardman's Plantation*

This plantation is dedicated to the memory of Fred Heardman, a legendary figure of the Peak District who was, for many years, the landlord of both the Old Nag's Head and the Church Inn (now the Rambler Inn). Known to his friends as Bill the Bogtrotter for his exploits on arduous walks and runs in the Peak, he became a rural district councillor and fought, fortunately very successfully, against the industrialization of this attractive valley. He was also a member of the Peak District Branch of the Council for the Preservation of Rural England, and when the Peak District National Park was formed, the Nag's Head became their first information centre and mountain rescue post.

3.24

BLEAKLOW FROM GLOSSOP

STARTING AND FINISHING
POINT
Old Glossop. Cars may be parked
beside factory (110-045948) on the
north-east outskirts of Glossop.
LENGTH
10 miles (16 km)
ASCENT
1450 ft (450 m)

There are three summits in the Peak District which achieve the magic height of 2000 ft (610 m) and two of these, Bleaklow Head and Higher Shelf Stones, are visited on this walk. The strangely-eroded shapes of Wain Stones, Hern Stones and Higher Shelf Stones on the high moors have attracted walkers for over a hundred years.

The ascent, up Torside Clough, along the Pennine Way, and the descent, down the reputed Roman road of Doctor's Gate, both follow good footpaths beside clear, sparkling mountain streams. This ascent of Bleaklow is both delightful and much easier underfoot than many of the alternative routes.

ROUTE DESCRIPTION (Maps 39–41)

From the parking place, turn L at the end of the factory and follow the road round until it meets Charles Lane, which doubles back up the hill to a stile. Passing a quarry the sunken lane goes uphill through three stiles to a fourth where the walls fan out. Turn half L following the L wall, and in 250 yards (225 m) strike directly up the hillside to a stile in the fence. A bearing of NE brings you to Glossop Low Quarries (1), a complex array of depressions and spoil heaps through which you should attempt to navigate a straight line to arrive at the OS trig point on the top of Cock Hill.

From the summit walk for about ½ mile (800 m) still on a NE bearing over rough grass and heather until a stony track is reached. Turn R along it to the ruined shooting cabin on Glossop Low. From the ruin follow a faint path, again heading NE, and in a few yards the Woodlands Valley comes into view. On the skyline are the twin Holme Moss television masts, and opposite can be seen Crowden Youth Hostel in the valley of Crowden Brook, which is for many walkers the end of a long, first day on the Pennine Way. The path leads across the moor for ¼ mile (400 m) until, quite suddenly and dramatically,

Opposite The Pennine Way looking towards Higher Shelf Stones

Torside Clough appears at your feet. The Pennine Way is joined at this point.

Turn R and follow Clough Edge on a level path, with the clough gradually climbing to meet it. After a mile (1.6 km) Wildboar Grain joins Torside Clough. Turn L, descending to cross the stream, and follow the path eastwards up the L bank. In ¾ mile (1.2 km), where the stream gradually disappears and the peat groughs become more evident, the path swings gradually R. Continue along the path and after a further ¼ mile (400 m) the cairn on Bleaklow Head is reached, surrounded by a sea of silver sand.

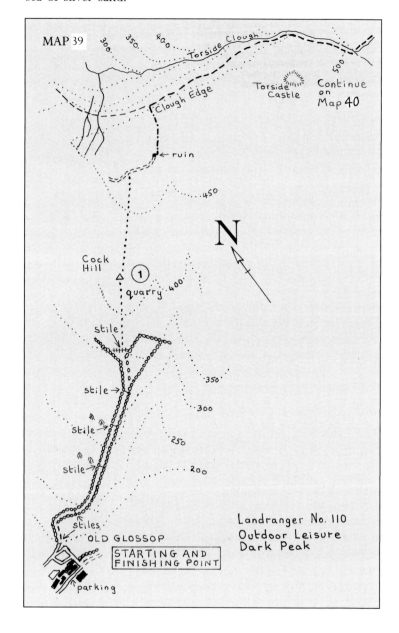

MAP 39

Landranger No. 110
Outdoor Leisure
Dark Peak

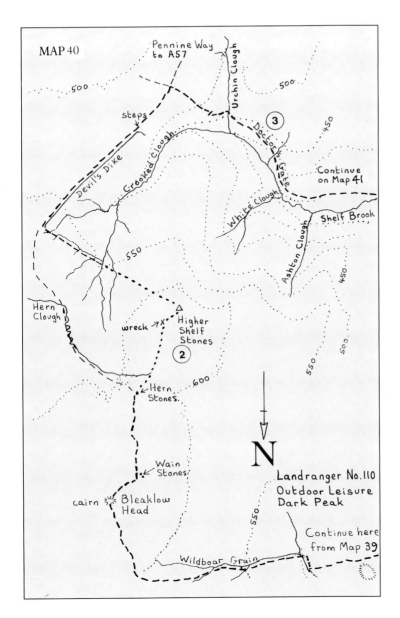

A solitary pole to the SW points to Wain Stones (known as 'The Kiss'), just out of sight but only 200 yards (180 m) away. From here in clear weather Hern Stones will be seen due S less than ½ mile (800 m) distant. The intervening ground is without a clear path although very many feet tread this way every weekend; the reason for this is the peat.

At Hern Stones the Pennine Way is left temporarily in order to visit Higher Shelf Stones *(2)*, the second of the 2000 ft (610 m) summits. This is reached after approximately ½ mile (800 m) on a SW bearing, but by aiming just L of the direct line to Higher Shelf Stones the wreckage of a Flying Fortress aircraft may be visited first.

The escarpment to the SW is Lower Shelf Stones with Glossop beyond, while Shelf Brook flows through the deep valley ahead. Now head SE towards a dyke near the head of Crooked Clough. Climb up this to rejoin the Pennine Way which follows Devil's Dike (probably an old boundary ditch). Turn R and in ½ mile (800 m) a flight of wooden steps is met at the end of a board walk built to minimize erosion. In ¼ mile (400 m) turn R at a crossing path (Doctor's Gate) *(3)* and descend past Urchin Clough to follow Shelf Brook towards Glossop (once known as Glott's Valley).

When the valley flattens out, a further ½ mile (800 m) brings you to the Memorial Footbridge across Shelf Brook. From here the boundary of open country lies ¾ mile (1.2 km) downstream where a track is joined coming in from the R by a barn. Go down this track to cross a stile and over the bridge ahead. The track is now followed through a gap and three gates; the last opens onto an unmetalled road which leads in ½ mile (800 m) back to Old Glossop.

1 Glossop Low Quarries

This quarry, which closed towards the end of the nineteenth century, was used as a source of local building stone, specializing in paving flags and roofing slabs. A rood of roofing slabs was 44 square yards (37 sq m) and cost 52 shillings at the quarry and 64 shillings in the town when the quarry was in its heyday. That the lane which leads up to the quarries on Cock Hill once took substantial traffic is evident from the gritstone paving slabs which may still be seen where they have not yet been covered by encroaching grass.

2 Higher Shelf Stones

This is typical Bleaklow; wild peat groughs (though not as deep as those of Kinder), no path and only the compass to guide you. In bad weather this is quite a frightening place to be; in good weather it is a fascinating area to visit. Bleaklow comes from the Old English meaning 'dark coloured hill'.

Very close to the OS trig point the remains of a Flying Fortress may be seen. The gleaming metal is scattered over a wide area almost as though the accident had only just happened; in fact the crash, in which thirteen American airmen died, occurred on 3 November 1948. Four engines and many metal fragments are scattered about and, although it is illegal to remove any pieces, at one time the entire fuselage and tail could be seen.

The rocks at Higher Shelf Stones are covered more than usual in graffiti, including an early example dating from 7 October 1871.

Old Woman, the view towards Bleaklow

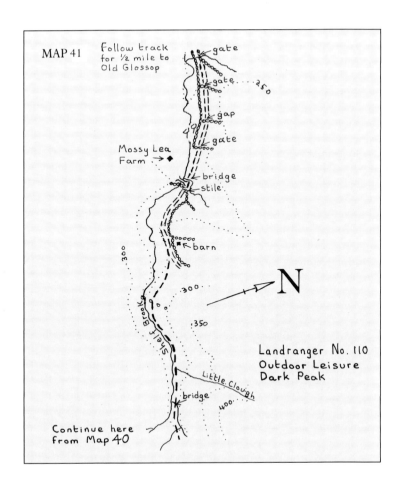

3 Doctor's Gate

Gate means road and since 1627 this track has been known as Doctor Talbotes Gate. Dr John Talbot, Vicar of Glossop, 1494-1550, was the illegitimate son of the Earl of Shrewsbury and may have used the old Roman road when visiting his father's castle in Sheffield. The Roman road, from the fort of Navio at Hope to that of Melandra at Glossop, led via Hope Cross, across Blackley Clough, past Hayridge Farm and Oyster Clough to the Snake Road. The next section over Coldharbour Moor, is the best preserved and shows how the road was constructed with slabs set on edge between kerbstones. As the track descends Shelf Brook, it becomes very eroded and loses its character. The road was used by packhorses until the construction of the turnpike in 1821.

1.25

THROUGH THE LLUGWY GORGE

STARTING POINT
Ty-hyll (the Ugly House) (115-756575)
FINISHING POINT
Pont-y-Pair bridge, Betws-y-Coed (115-792567)
LENGTH
2¾ miles (4.5 km)
ASCENT
100 ft (30 m)

An extremely attractive walk along the Llugwy Gorge past the Ugly House, the Swallow Falls and the Miners' Bridge, including a stretch of the Gwydyr Forest. The Swallow Falls are probably the most popular tourist attraction in Wales, but almost everybody else will be on the opposite bank, where a charge is made for admission.

ROUTE DESCRIPTION (Map 42)

From the Ugly House *(1)*, cross the minor road and pass the small private car-park to the end of the bridge (PFS). Go down the steps on to the river bank and walk downstream with the river to the R, soon crossing a stile into a wood. The path continues in the same direction, gradually rising above the river until the Swallow Falls *(2)* can be seen below. A superb path runs across the steep wooded hillside above the falls with rocks above and a steep fall down to the R towards the river. Despite this spectacular setting, however, there is no real danger as a guarding fence has been erected throughout.

Where the fence ends, reach open ground. The wide path to the L goes to the tea-gardens at Allt-isaf which can be used for a pleasant break. Otherwise, continue in the same direction along a narrow path crossing a small stream and through a plantation of young trees. After the plantation take the wide path which rises through mature trees to a forest track at the top *(3)*. Here turn R to a road where turn R again. After about 50 yards (45 m) drop down to the R on to a lower and extremely pleasant path through the forest. The path is level to start with, but later descends steeply towards the river; carry on, crossing two small bridges near the river, until a splendid fenced viewpoint is reached overlooking rapids. Rise L up to the road.

Go R along the road for about 60 yards (55 m), then leave the road to the R dropping down by a fence to the Miners' Bridge *(4)*. Do not cross, but continue downstream on the same side of

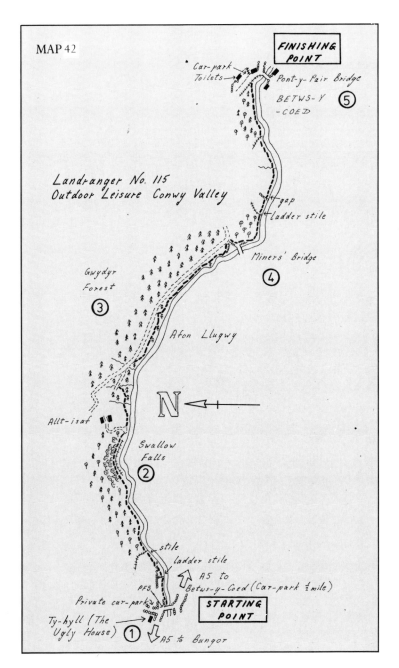

MAP 42

FINISHING POINT

Car-park
Toilets

Pont-y-Pair Bridge

BETWS-Y -COED (5)

Landranger No. 115
Outdoor Leisure Conwy Valley

gap
ladder stile

Miners' Bridge (4)

Gwydyr Forest (3)

Afon Llugwy

N ←

Allt-isaf

Swallow Falls (2)

stile
ladder stile

A5 to Betws-y-Coed (Car-park ½ mile)

PFS

Private car-park

STARTING POINT

Ty-hyll (The Ugly House) (1)

A5 to Bangor

the river, soon leaving the wood over a ladder stile. Continue along the bank, later crossing a fence, until a road is reached opposite the car-park at the Pont-y-Pair bridge *(5)* at Betws-y-Coed.

1 Ty-hyll, the Ugly House

The Ugly House, which stands on the Capel Curig side of the bridge over the Llugwy, lives up to its name. A rough and primitive building of enormous strength, with slate roof and walls of unusual thickness, it was built about 1475. No mortar was used.

2 *The Swallow Falls*

A survey in 1975 showed that the Swallow Falls were visited by about 690,000 people annually. The majority of visitors approach the Falls from the road on the south side, where a car-park has been provided, paying a fee for the privilege. The Falls can also be viewed from the north bank, free of charge, using the public right-of-way; here the view is admittedly poorer but the walking much more exciting.

George Borrow, who visited North Wales in 1854 and wrote of his experiences in *Wild Wales*, which is now a classic still sold in local shops, described the Falls as follows: 'The Fall of the Swallow is not a majestic single fall, but a succession of small ones. First there are a number of little foaming torrents, bursting through rocks about twenty yards above the promontory, on which I stood. Then came two beautiful rolls of white water, dashing into a pool a little way above the promontory; then there is a swirl of water round its corner into a pool below on its right, black as death and seemingly of great depth; then a rush through a very narrow outlet into another pool, from which the water clamours away down the glen. Such is the Rhaiadr y Wennol, or Swallow Fall; called so from the rapidity with which the waters rush and skip along'.

3 *The Gwydyr Forest*

The walk passes through a lovely section of the forest, the property of the Forestry Commission.

4 *The Miners' Bridge*

The Miners' Bridge over the Llugwy is inclined as a ladder from one bank to the other at an angle of about 30° to the horizontal. The bridge originally served as a convenient route for miners living nearby at Pentre-du, south of the river, to reach their work in the lead mines situated on the higher ground to the north. The present bridge was erected about 1983 and is the fifth or sixth on the site.

5 *Pont-y-Pair Bridge, Betws-y-Coed*

'The Bridge of the Cauldron', spanning the turbulent Llugwy by a series of five arches at the western end of Betws-y-Coed, is of uncertain date. It may be fifteenth century, built by a local man named Howel, but it may also be the work of Inigo Jones about 200 years later in the seventeenth. There are fine rapids upstream from the bridge — hence its name.

Afon Llugwy

To the Rhaeadr-fawr, The Aber Falls

Bontnewydd (115-662720). From A55, turn up minor road in Aber by Aber Falls Hotel and Garage, and immediately R (sign on road). Continue up road for about ¼ mile (1.2 km) to small car-park by bridge over river; there is a further and larger car-park across the bridge.

LENGTH
3 miles (5 km)
ASCENT
500 ft (150 m)

A short but exceedingly pleasant walk which follows the river to the Rhaeadr-fawr, a spectacular waterfall 120 ft (37 m) high. Return by the same route or by a delightful path through a coniferous forest.

Route Description (Map 43)

From the small car-park by the bridge over the Afon Aber go through the small gate to the L of the Park Information Board *(1)* (footpath sign to Aber Falls). Keep on the R side of the stream to a footbridge, cross and go through the gate on the far side into the farm road beyond. Turn R along the farm road and continue ahead, ignoring the farm road bending back to the L. Further along, bend round to the R of a small cottage. Soon after the cottage, where the farm road goes L and becomes faint, go ahead on a path through a gap in a wall and later through a gate. The falls are now directly ahead.

You can return, of course, by the same route but a much better way is to use a lovely woodland path which crosses the hillside to the R and which will give about the same distance. For this alternative path return to the gate, go through, then turn R over a ladder stile and climb away from the falls up the slope half L along the obvious path (the path is marked by short posts with blue painted tops). Eventually at the end of the rise go over a stile into a wood and follow the path ahead, keeping L at a path junction (do not follow the blue markers here, which are for the R-hand path). This delightful path through the forest is quite clear throughout. Eventually leave the wood over a stile and on through a wall gap to the R of a sheepfold. Continue in the same direction with a fence to your R to reach the farm road that you walked along earlier on your way to the falls. Turn R along it back to the car-park.

The Aber Falls in winter

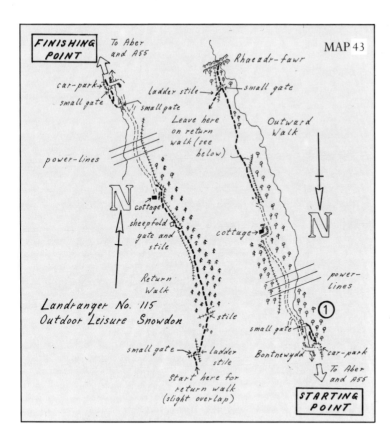

1 Coedydd Aber National Nature Reserve

The valley of the Afon Rhaeadr Fawr as far as the Aber Falls, the hilltop of Maes y Gaer and a small strip along the Afon Anafon together form the Reserve set up by the Nature Conservancy Council in 1975. Its main interest lies in its woodland of broad-leaved trees, mainly oak, a remnant of the great forests that once covered most of the valleys and the lower hillsides of North Wales.

Coedydd Aber Nature Trail, Nature Conservancy Council.

Bontnewydd. The starting point for Route 26.

2.27

THE TRAVERSE OF THE GLYDER RIDGE

STARTING AND FINISHING POINT
Ogwen (115-649603), on the A5 from Capel Curig to Bethesda.
LENGTH
$5\frac{1}{2}$ miles (9 km)
ASCENT
2375 ft (720 m)

The great ridge of Glyder Fach and Glyder Fawr is reached from Ogwen by a path that ascends near the outfall of Llyn Bochlwyd before striking over to the wild col of Bwlch Tryfan. The final ascent to the summit ridge is across and up steep scree. The summits themselves, with their huge and weird towers of weathered rock, are the most unusual in Snowdonia. The return to Ogwen is down exceptionally steep scree slopes to the west of the Fawr, followed by a spectacular descent to the foot of the Devil's Kitchen. A short route, but one of the finest mountain expeditions in Snowdonia for the moderate walker.

ROUTE DESCRIPTION (Maps 44, 45)

Start in the car-park by the Youth Hostel at Ogwen. Leave the car-park along a well-maintained path from the far corner; this crosses a fence and a footbridge and rises up the hillside. Where the path bends R, do not turn with it but continue in the same direction as before along a faint path, heading for some waterfalls, the Bochlwyd Falls, which can be seen on the hillside ahead. Work has been done on this path recently which climbs on the R-hand side of the falls. At the top, cross over to the opposite bank and continue on the path around the L shore of a lake, Llyn Bochlwyd. The path then rises and bends to the L to reach the Bwlch Tryfan, a magnificent col between Tryfan and Glyder Fach.

Cross the wall by one of the ladder stiles and turn R to climb up the steep hillside. The path climbs up the scree to the L of the rocks ahead (Bristly Ridge), to reach the top. Continue across the top to the prominent pile of huge slabs ahead *(1)*. Further along, reach the summit of Glyder Fach, which is the second pile of slabs, and further still the weird spires of rock, which are known as the Castle of the Winds.

Do not attempt to pass this on the R-hand side where there is a considerable drop, use instead a path that descends on the L

158

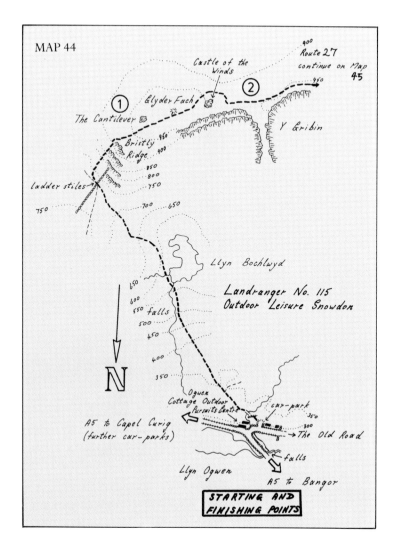

MAP 44

Route 27
continue on Map
45

Castle of the
Winds

Glyder Fach

① The Cantilever

② Y Gribin

Bristly
Ridge

ladder stiles

750

Llyn Bochlwyd

**Landranger No. 115
Outdoor Leisure Snowdon**

falls

N

Ogwen
Cottage Outdoor
Pursuits Centre

car-park

A5 to Capel Curig
(further car-parks)

→ The Old Road

falls

Llyn Ogwen

A5 to Bangor

**STARTING AND
FINISHING POINTS**

and then rises again beyond. The path from here to Glyder Fawr *(2) (3) (4)*, slightly to the L of the ridge top, is very clear and well-marked with cairns. The prominent pile of rocks at the far end marks the summit. The path continues in the same direction for a short distance beyond the summit, before turning to the R and dropping down very steep scree well-marked with cairns. Continue down to the grassy col by Llyn y Cŵn.

When you reach the grassy slopes of the col from the scree, turn sharp R to cross an area of marshy ground past a prominent cairn to pick up a path. Follow this path down a small valley, well-marked with cairns, eventually meeting a small stream. *Do not follow the stream down as it goes over a considerable cliff.* Instead, bend to the L down a shelf following the base of the cliff, to the bottom of the Devil's Kitchen *(5)*. Cross the stream at the base of the Kitchen and descend the boulder slope on the L-hand side, eventually reaching a path that will lead you around the L-

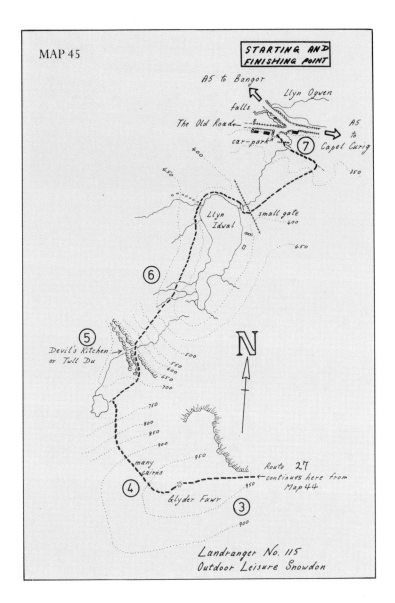

MAP 45

STARTING AND
FINISHING POINT

A5 to Bangor

Llyn Ogwen

falls

The Old Roade

A5 to Capel Curig

car-park

⑦

350

400

450

Llyn Idwal

small gate

400

450

⑥

⑤

Devil's Kitchen
or Twll Du

500

550
600
650
700

N

750

800

850

900

950

many cairns

Route 27
—continues here from Map 44

950

④

Glyder Fawr

③

900

Landranger No. 115
Outdoor Leisure Snowdon

hand side of Llyn Idwal *(6)*. At the far end of the lake cross a footbridge and go through a gate in a fence; then follow the clear path beyond down to Ogwen *(7)*.

1 The Cantilever

The huge horizontal slab of rock about 25 ft (7.5 m) long, with at least 9 ft (2.7 m) projecting into space, a short distance north of the summit of Glyder Fach, is known as the Cantilever. It is one of the most photographed sights in Snowdonia. Thomas Pennant, who visited North Wales in

Bristly Ridge, Glyder Fach

1778, included a drawing of the Cantilever in his book *Tour of Wales*, looking remarkably the same as it does today. It is highly likely that walkers two centuries hence will find it still in place.

2 *Dyffryn Mymbyr*

The farm of Dyffryn Mymbyr, situated roughly mid-way between Capel Curig and the Pen-y-Gwryd by the Llynnau Mymbyr, was the scene of Thomas Firbank's best-selling book *I Bought a Mountain*. Firbank was a Canadian by birth, but had been educated in England and had spent his holidays on a farm in Merionethshire. In 1931 he returned to England and bought a sheep farm of 2400 acres (970 ha) with its stock of 1300 sheep, where he stayed until the war came in 1939. *I Bought a Mountain* is the story of his eight years on the Welsh hill-farm. The mountainside of Glyder Fach was part of the farm, hence the title.

The book, first published in 1940, was an immediate best-seller and still sells well today; it is usually on sale in shops within the Park.

3 *The Marching Camp at Pen-y-Gwryd*

By AD 74, some thirty years after the Romans had landed upon the British shore at Richborough in Kent, the frontier of the Roman Empire had been pushed to a line corresponding roughly to that of modern Wales. Three great legionary fortresses had been built at Chester, Wroxeter and Caerleon, but it is unlikely that the frontier was ever wholly peaceful, and campaigns against the Welsh tribes were mounted by Scapula between AD 47 and 52, by Veranius in 57 and by Paulinus in 58 and 59. The final conquest was not achieved however until AD 75 when Frontinus defeated the tribe of the Silures in South Wales and AD 78 when Agricola conquered the Ordovices of North Wales. But from then onwards for 400 years Wales was an integral part of the Roman Empire.

The main line of advance of the Roman army probably took place over high ground, as the river valleys would be covered by dense forest and difficult to negotiate. When the invading army stopped it would erect a temporary camp, now referred to as a marching camp. Here the legionnaires would throw up an earth wall, 5–6 ft high (1.5–1.8 m), upon which they would erect a palisade of stakes to give greater protection. Inside, tents of leather would be laid out in regular order.

The valley and slopes to the left of the Glyder Ridge mark one of the lines of advance of the Roman Army, and by the Pen-y-Gwryd Hotel is the site of a marching camp, the only one known in North Wales at the present time.

Glyder Fawr

4 *The Pen-y-Gwryd Hotel*

This famous hotel stands at the junction of the roads to Llanberis, Capel Curig and Beddgelert about 1 mile (1.6 km) from Pen-y-Pass. Originally a farmhouse owned by John Roberts of Llanberis, it became an inn when Henry Owen decided to take out a licence in 1847, and with his wife, Ann, was to stay there as landlord for forty-four years until his death in 1891. In his time the inn grew in importance and became the Home of Mountaineering in North Wales. It declined somewhat after about 1900 due to the influence of Owen Rawson Owen at the Gorphwysfa, but since 1947 it has resumed its original standing and is today one of the great centres of British mountaineering.

Pen-y-Gwryd has always been a base for Everest expeditions and in 1953 the team for the successful expedition stayed there for part of their training. The Everest Room at the hotel carries on its ceiling the signatures of members of the expedition, and in the residents' private room there is a case containing souvenirs of the expedition including samples of rock from the summit and a length of the rope which linked Hilary and Tensing during their final climb. Since 1953, a reunion of expedition members has been held every five years at the Pen-y-Gwryd.

5 *The Devil's Kitchen*

A magnificent view down into the Kitchen can be obtained by following the outflow from Llyn y Cŵn as far as a small grassy platform above the cleft. Afterwards, retrace your steps back to Llyn y Cŵn to continue the descent as described.

6 *Llyn Idwal*

The low hills by the lake on the return leg are moraines left there by the glacier during the Ice Age. The lake itself has a certain sinister reputation, for legend has it that a young Prince Idwal was deliberately drowned there. For that reason, it is said, no bird will fly over the water.

7 *Ogwen*

Do not leave Ogwen without a visit to the falls and a short walk down the Old Road for a superb view of the Nant Ffrancon Pass. The best view can be obtained from the Old Road just beyond the Youth Hostel. On the left are the hanging valleys of Cwm Bual, Cwm Perfedd, Cwm Graianog and Cwm Ceunant, ahead is the Nant Ffrancon with its flat floor of green fields over which the Afon Ogwen meanders and to the right is the steep face of Penyrole-wen and of the western Carneddau. The old Penrhyn road can be seen running along the left-hand side of the valley and on the right-hand side is the present A5 which also marks the old line of Telford's Turnpike.

View from the Miners' Track near Glyder Fach (the Pen-y-Gwryd Hotel is left of centre at the junction of the three roads)

THE PONY TRACK TO PENYGADAIR (NORTHERN ROUTE)

STARTING AND FINISHING
POINT
Ty-nant car-park (124-698153).
Leave Dolgellau along the A493
towards the toll bridge and Tywyn.
Fork L on minor road. The car-park is
on R after 2½ miles (4 km). There is
a small information point nearby
which is open in summer.
LENGTH
5 miles (8 km)
ASCENT
2400 ft (730 m)

A short and straightforward route to the summit of Cader Idris,
except for the final ascent where the path rises more steeply
over rougher ground along the edge of a deep and impressive
cwm with a considerable drop to the left. The track has been
extensively repaired and well-marked with signs and cairns
throughout, and no difficulty will be found in following it. The
views, particularly from the final summit ridge, are magnificent.
Return by the same route.

ROUTE DESCRIPTION (Map 46)

Walk from the car-park into the road and turn R. At a telephone
box (PFS) turn L over a stile and go up the farm road beyond soon
passing a farm. After the farm, continue ahead through a gate,
over a small bridge and uphill with a stream and wood on the L.
At a footpath sign turn R, leaving the farm road through a gap,
and go between two walls, soon bending L to a small gate. After
the gate the path bends R over a small stream and then L uphill
through a gap to a small gate in a wall. Continue up the hill
moving R to a further wall with a small gate. Go through the gate
and follow a path with a wall on the R.

Where the wall bends away, the path rises steeply up the
ridge ahead through zig-zags, eventually passing through a gap
and a stile (Rhiw Gwredydd). From the stile the path goes half L
keeping near to the fence on the L. Where the fence turns to the
L continue ahead up steps following a line of cairns. The path
goes up the mountainside gradually approaching the lip of a
great cliff dropping L into the depths of an impressive cwm,
with Llyn y Gadair far below. Continue along the path on the
edge of the cliff rising steeply to the summit of Penygadair.

Return by the same route back to Ty-nant.

Opposite Cader Idris

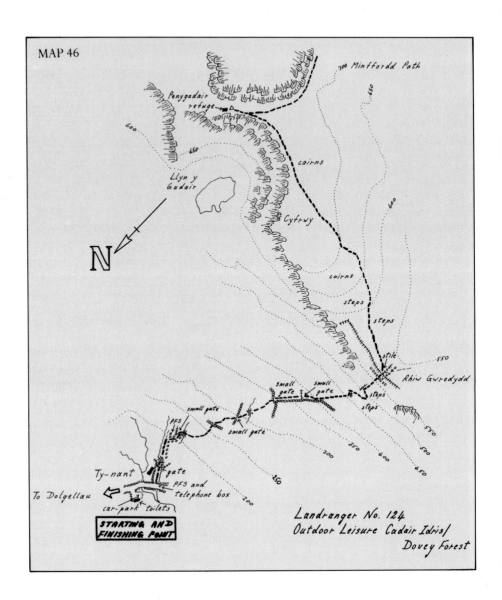

MAP 46

Mintfordd Path

Penygadair
refuge

cairns

Llyn y
Gadair

Cyfrwy

N

cairns

steps

steps

stile

Rhiw Gwredydd

small
gate

small
gate

steps

small gate

steps

small gate

PFS

Ty-nant
gate

To Dolgellau

PFS and
telephone box

car-park toilets

STARTING AND
FINISHING POINT

Landranger No. 124
Outdoor Leisure Cadair Idris/
Dovey Forest

3.29

THE NANTLLE RIDGE

This is one of the finest ridge walks in North Wales, ranking with the Snowdon Horseshoe and the ridge of the Carneddau. Its eastern end is well-frequented but the western summits, being more isolated, are usually lonely. There are a few stretches of scrambling, but these can usually be avoided by taking easier lines nearby. The views from the ridge, into Cwm Pennant on the left and the Nantlle valley on the right, are remarkable.

ROUTE DESCRIPTION (Maps 47–49)

Walk from the car-park at Rhyd-ddu (1) into the road (A4085) and cross to a small gate on the opposite side (PFS). Take the R-hand path towards a farm which soon reaches a bridge. Do not cross, but turn L along the river bank to a second bridge. Cross this bridge; after a stile go half R to a farm road and follow this to the R to reach a gate leading into a road (PFS). Do not go through the gate, but instead turn L through a small gate and follow a path with a wall on the R. At a fence (after bends on the wall) go through a gap and turn L with the fence on the L. Where the fence bends away L, continue up the mountainside to a ladder stile and then to a large boulder marked with white arrows. Take the R-hand path (sign 'Ridge') steeply uphill (faint white arrows) to a further ladder stile. The path continues up to reach still another ladder stile in a wall on the ridge top. Cross to the summit cairn of Y Garn.

Return to the ladder stile and, after crossing, turn R to follow the ridge with the wall to the R. Later, cross the wall to follow a path near to the edge. (The route along the edge has some exciting moments with magnificent views down the considerable cliff to the R. An alternative route may be followed, however, just down from the crest to the L, which cuts out both the exciting moments and the views.) Reach the top of Mynydd Drws-y-coed and cross a ladder stile in a fence. Continue along the ridge to the summit of Trum y Ddysgl and then descend approximately south-west down a grassy ridge. After about 300 yards (275 m) branch R approximately due east to descend a

STARTING POINT
Rhyd-ddu (115-571526), 3½ miles (5.5 km) from Beddgelert along the Caernarfon road (A4085)

FINISHING POINT
Nebo (115-479505), about 1 mile (1.6 km) east of the Porthmadog-Caernarfon road (A487)

LENGTH
7½ miles (12 km)

ASCENT
2988 ft (910 m)

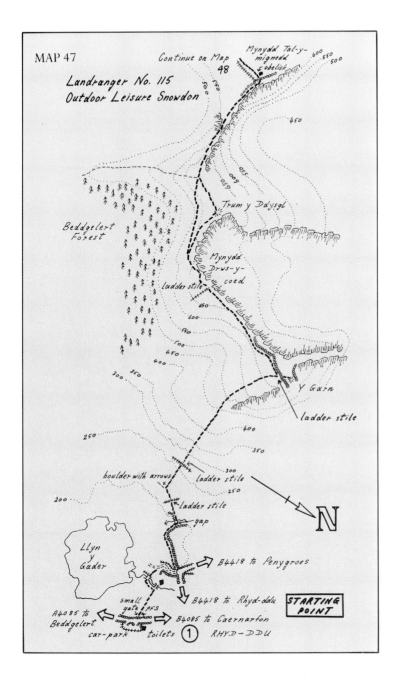

MAP 47

Landranger No. 115
Outdoor Leisure Snowdon

Continue on Map 48

Mynydd Tal-y-mignedd
obelisk

Beddgelert Forest

Trum y Ddysgl

Mynydd Drws-y-coed

ladder stile

Y Garn

ladder stile

boulder with arrows

ladder stile

ladder stile

gap

N

Llyn y Gader

B4418 to Penygroes

B4418 to Rhyd-ddu

STARTING POINT

small gate & PFS

A4085 to Beddgelert

B4085 to Caernarfon

car-park   toilets ① RHYD-DDU

narrow grass ridge which gradually becomes still narrower, until a collapsed section is reached. Cross and climb the ridge beyond to the large obelisk on Mynydd Tal-y-mignedd.

From the obelisk continue down a ridge to the L (i.e. SW) with a fence to the L. Follow the clear path by the fence eventually to descend steeply into the col of Bwlch Dros-bern (crossing and re-crossing the fence at ladder stiles). At the far side of the col where the wall (i.e. at the end of the fence) reaches a rock face, scramble up the rocks at a convenient point

Opposite *Looking back from the lower slopes of Y Garn over Llyn y Gader*

171

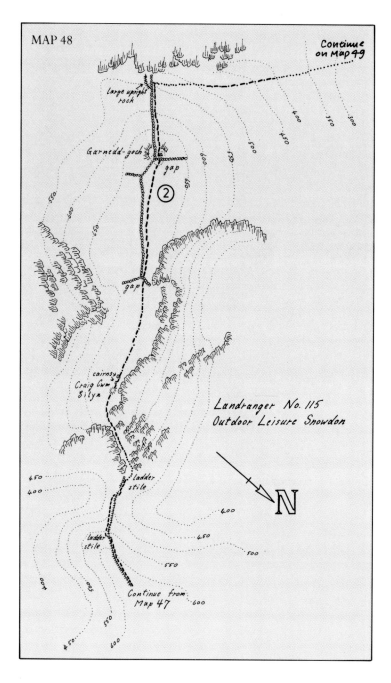

MAP 48

Continue on Map 49

large upright rock

Garnedd-goch

gap

②

gap

cairns
Craig Cwm Silyn

Landranger No. 115
Outdoor Leisure Snowdon

N

ladder stile

ladder stile

Continue from Map 47

to pick up a path at the top. Continue up the ridge beyond, to reach the large summit cairn of Craig Cwm Silyn, and then along the top of the ridge, past two prominent cairns, to a wall. Go through a gap and then on in the same direction with the wall to the L to reach a gap in a further wall. The OS obelisk of Garnedd-goch *(2)* is just over the wall on the opposite side.

View SSW from Y Garn on the Nantlle Ridge

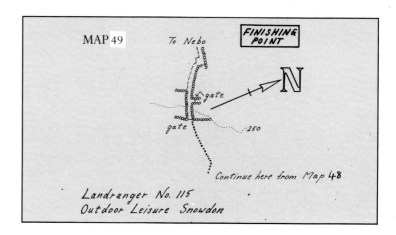

Beyond the obelisk continue in the same direction now descending with the wall still on the L; where the hillside steepens (a fence begins by a tall rock on the opposite side of the wall) turn R to contour the hillside. The path is faint at first but improves later and is waymarked by short upright stones. Descend to a large moorland area to the R of a lake and cross to an obvious walled lane on the opposite side. Enter the lane by a gate and follow it to its end where it bends R to a road. Follow the road to Nebo.

1 *Welsh Highland Railway*

The railway followed the A4085 closely on its eastern side from near Pitt's Head to Rhyd-ddu, north of which it went further to the east along a winding track past Llyn Cwellyn. There were stations by the present Snowdon Ranger Youth Hostel and at the car-park at Rhyd-ddu.

2 *Slate Quarries in the Nantlle Valley*

The Nantlle Valley was the scene of some of the biggest slate quarries in North Wales, although not on the scale of those at Llanberis and Bethesda. The slate was extracted from open pits in the valley floor. The biggest were the Dorothea, which worked from about 1829, the Penyrorsedd from about 1816 and the Talysarn. The quarries can be easily seen from the crest of the Nantlle Ridge about the summit of Garnedd-goch.

1.30

MERRIVALE—KING'S TOR—SWELL TOR AND FOGGIN TOR

STARTING AND FINISHING
POINT
Car-park in a roadside quarry on L
side of B3357, as approach
Merrivale Bridge from Princetown
(191-553750); 3 miles (5 km) west
of Two Bridges, 4½ miles (7.2 km)
east of Tavistock.
LENGTH
4 miles (6.5 km)
ASCENT
Mostly level walking between
1050–1312 ft (320–400 m) above
sea level.

This walk allows an exploration of the prehistoric stone rows, stone circle, cairns and standing stone on Long Ash Hill, which together represent one of the finest groups of ancient monuments on Dartmoor. The walk follows for much of its length the now-closed Yelverton to Princetown Railway which was built in 1881 along the trackbed of an earlier line—a horse-truck tramway (the Plymouth and Dartmoor Railway) used for transporting granite from the quarries.

ROUTE DESCRIPTION (Map 50)

From the east end of the car-park, walking with your back to Merrivale Quarry, head off over the moor, half R, in the direction of North Hessary Tor mast. After some 250 yards (229 m) head half R again over the crest of Long Ash Hill. A prehistoric sanctuary (1) comprising kistvaens, a stone circle, a menhir, cairns and three stone rows—two double and one single—comes into view.

Keeping to the L of the rows cross over a leat via a small granite slab to prevent bank erosion. Follow the southern double stone row down, almost due west, to its far end—a distance of some 280 yards (256 m). From here go half L passing a cairn circle, and go to the stone circle and the fine menhir.

From the menhir bear L keeping the boundary wall to the R. Follow a path keeping above (L) of the bluff for a short distance and then cut down R to follow a path through the tinners' spoil heaps keeping the stream on the R; the going can be boggy here. Cross the stream (the Pila Brook) by the ford and follow the boundary wall on the R up the slope. Where the wall bends markedly to the R continue straight on up the hill to pick up the track bed of the former Yelverton and Princetown Railway,

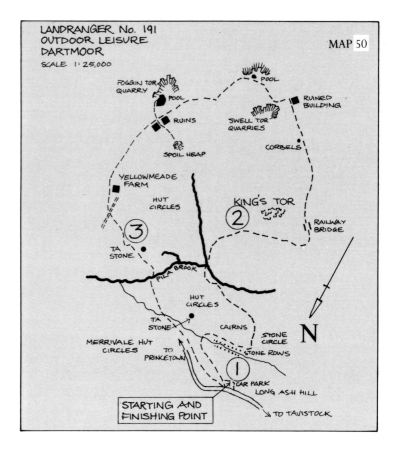

LANDRANGER No. 191
OUTDOOR LEISURE
DARTMOOR
SCALE 1:25,000

MAP 50

FOGGIN TOR
QUARRY
POOL

POOL

RUINED
BUILDING

RUINS

SWELL TOR
QUARRIES

CORBELS

SPOIL HEAP

YELLOWMEADE
FARM

HUT
CIRCLES

KING'S TOR

RAILWAY
BRIDGE

TA
STONE

PILA BROOK

HUT
CIRCLES

TA
STONE

CAIRNS

STONE
CIRCLE

MERRIVALE HUT
CIRCLES

TO
PRINCETOWN

STONE ROWS

N

CAR PARK
LONG ASH HILL

TO TAVISTOCK

STARTING AND
FINISHING POINT

which was built for most of its length on an earlier line, the Plymouth and Dartmoor Railway (P & DR) *(2)*.

The track forks as it swings L round King's Tor; here take the R fork along the P & DR for extensive views over the Walkham valley. Follow the track round to the L and, on approaching a fine granite railway bridge, cross over the Yelverton and Princetown Railway track and turn R for Swell Tor Sidings. Continue straight on along this track bed to Swelltor Quarries passing abandoned granite corbels on the L. On this track are many sleepers, some with their retaining bolts—watch where you put your feet. On reaching a ruined building (R), opposite the mouth of the quarry, turn L uphill keeping the quarry entrance down on the L. Keep over to the R to avoid encountering the quarry edge. On reaching the first level half way up the hill bear R passing the spoil heaps radiating out from the side of the tor. Continue along the track here bending round to the L, passing two smaller quarries (one water-filled) and their accompanying spoil heaps on the R. If the weather should become misty, to avoid climbing above Swelltor Quarries continue straight on along the track from the ruined building and contour L round the hillside.

Left: *Abandoned granite corbels near Swell Tor sidings.*

Following page: *Foggintor Quarries. Several considerable ruins still survive.*

Go along the track in the direction of Foggintor Quarries; granite sleepers with bolts can be seen along this stretch. Where the track and a path intersect, turn R and follow the path towards the quarries. On reaching the Yelverton and Princetown Railway track in a shallow cutting, cut straight across and continue on the path. At the next track bear L and go to the ruined buildings. At the largest ruin on the L, with its massive granite blockwork, bear L passing between the two walls of the building and follow the spoil heap to its far end, being wary of ironwork jutting slightly out of the ground at regular intervals. The views west and north include King's Tor, Cox Tor, Long Ash Hill, Staple Tors, Roos Tor and Great Mis Tor. Below lies Yellowmeade Farm. Retrace your steps to the track and cut straight over following the path leading into the quarry, the sheer sides of which reflect in a small lake. The quarry can be explored by following the path round to the L. Here is the stillness of abandonment; echoes of blasting, chiselling, hauling and the voices of quarrymen have given way once more to raven croak and buzzard mew.

Retrace your steps and go R along the track and pass Yellowmeade Farm (on L). On reaching the final stone-walled enclosure on the L continue straight on for about 20 yards (18 m) beyond the junction with the farm track and bear L. Pass an oval-shaped prehistoric enclosure and go straight on downslope to a standing stone which marks a medieval route across Dartmoor (3). Go half R and continue on in the direction of Four Winds—an isolated clump of beech trees which used to be the site of a school serving quarry workers' children. Cross over the tinning gullies and then a small stream—it may be necessary to walk upstream to cross over safely. Continue on

over the hill, in the direction of Great Staple Tor, keeping Four Winds on the R. Cross over the leat where appropriate and keeping this well on the L continue in the same direction until approaching the stone rows once more. From here bear half R in the direction of Merrivale Quarry. With a Tavistock to Ashburton marker stone immediately on the L, in line with King's Tor, go half R passing some large prehistoric hut circles and inside one of the low-walled prehistoric enclosures is a granite apple crusher abandoned by the hand that made it, possibly because of an unacceptable flaw. Continue straight on in the direction of Merrivale Quarry to return to the car-park.

1 Long Ash Hill Prehistoric Monuments
The prehistoric monuments on the level plain of Long Ash Hill, near Merrivale may be a prehistoric sanctuary used for burials and ceremonies by several generations. Two double stone rows set 30 yards (27.4 m) apart run parallel to each other in an almost east–west orientation. These rows thus form a prehistoric 'avenue'—a unique feature on Dartmoor.

2 The Plymouth and Dartmoor Railway
The Plymouth and Dartmoor Railway (P & DR) was the brainchild of Sir Thomas Tyrwhitt. He was private secretary to George, Prince Regent, and was granted lands on Dartmoor in the Princetown area by the Prince in 1785. His ambition was to transform the high plateaux of Dartmoor, which in his eyes appeared as useless waste, into a vast prairie growing cereals and grass. He founded the community of Prince's Town (now Princetown) at a height of about 1345 feet (410 m) above sea level, and in 1819 he submitted a tramroad plan to Plymouth Chamber of Commerce and royal assent for this horse-driven railroad was given in 1821. This was to be Devon's first iron railroad and was opened on 26 September 1823.

3 A medieval road
A medieval trans-moorland packhorse track from Tavistock to Ashburton remained in use down the centuries until it was superseded by the turnpike road of 1792. Inscribed guide-posts—so-called 'T and A Stones'—were erected along the route, the initials 'T' and 'A' facing the appropriate town. By an Act of Parliament dated 1696 justices could enforce the erection of guide stones on roads; the 'T' and 'A' stones were sponsored in 1699 by Plymouth Corporation, which paid £2 for them to be put up, to help those travelling over Dartmoor find their way towards the city. These stones may have replaced an earlier series.

1.31

SHIPLEY BRIDGE—AVON DAM—EASTERN WHITE BARROW—BLACK TOR

STARTING AND FINISHING POINT
Shipley Bridge (202-681629). Large car-park; information board and toilets. 2½ miles (4 km) north north west of South Brent. Narrow lane approach, proceed with caution.

LENGTH
4½ miles (7 km)

ASCENT
One steep climb: 1 mile (1.5 km), ascent 505 ft (154 m) from the Avon Dam to Eastern White Barrow.

This walk, of moderate length, collides with the twentieth century on its approach to the Avon Dam and meets with more subtle exploitation of the moorland in the form of a prehistoric farmstead and village. For the second half of its length this is a high moorland walk and it should not be attempted in bad weather.

ROUTE DESCRIPTION (Map 51)

From the car-park pass the toilet block (on L) and continue straight on along the Water Authority access road (vehicular access to authorized vehicles only) northwards following the River Avon (on R) upstream. Within a short distance, just before a side road leads off and back to the L to the Avon Filtration Works is an inscribed granite block—the Hunters' Stone *(1)* on L. Continue upstream along the road passing the grounds and foundations of Brent Moor House (L) *(2)*. From here the road emerges out into open country flanked by Black Tor on the L and Dockwell Ridge on the R. Cross over the road bridge to continue on up the valley with the river now on the L. On the approach to Woolholes the valley bottom becomes flatter and broader. The river soon becomes confined again in Long-a-Traw where legend has it that a certain John Dill, a small-time smuggler, jumped the river here on horseback, while being pursued by the farmer from whom he had taken the horse.

Avon Dam now lies ahead *(3)*. The road here bears L crossing back over the river; follow the road to its end at the dam. Continue half L up the steep slope to the western end of the dam and, from here, go L heading straight on up the slope over open moorland keeping the reservoir down on the R. Soon, the

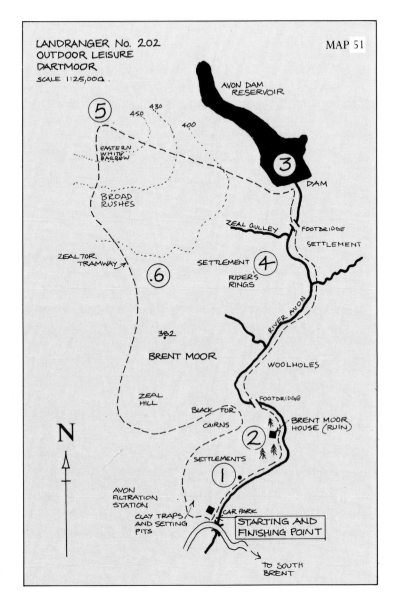

Above: *The Avon Dam.*

Following page: *A china clay settling pit above Shipley Bridge.*

huge—almost submarine-like—shape of Eastern White Barrow comes into view, but also notice beyond Zeal Gulley the prehistoric settlement of Rider's Rings *(4)*. Continue straight on for the prehistoric burial mound *(5)*.

From this summit go half L down the hill over Broad Rushes, keeping the headwater of the Bala Brook on the R. Head for a marked track running down the hillside. Turn L onto the track which is the trackbed of the nineteenth-century Zeal Tor Tramway in which peat was brought down from the moor to Shipley Bridge in horse-drawn trucks, and, which was later in the same century used to facilitate china clay extraction at Petre's Pit at the head of the Bala Brook *(6)*. Continue on down the track until Black Tor is immediately on the L and the confluence of the Middle Brook and the Bala Brook is on the R. Go L straight over the plain to Black Tor passing a mound—a ruined cairn—en route.

Go back half R from the tor passing a group of stones on the L which comprise a prehistoric settlement of hut circles and pound set within its own field system. Continue straight on until the Water Works filtration plant is visible. Descend to the Water Works road, cross over, and follow the path beside the wall (R) and then go L to explore the rectangular and circular pits which once served a clayworks here. Continue on down the slope to the road and car-park keeping a ruined building on the L. On either side of the road are further remains of the former clayworks which adopted the site of an abandoned peat-distilling works.

1 The Hunters' Stone

Mohun Harris who resided at Brent Moor House towards the end of the nineteenth century instigated the Hunters' Stone in memory of past huntsmen and Masters of Foxhounds of the Dartmoor Hunt. The Shipley Bridge area was one of the many Meets of the Hunt. The first inscriptions on the rock were the work of Billy Knott, a sculptor and fiddler, and include the names of 'Paul Treby', 'Trelawney', 'Bulteel' and 'Carew', together with Mohun Harris's initials. Paul Treby was never a Master of the Hunt but ran his own hounds from near Plympton in the eighteenth century. He did, however, give his hounds to Mr John Bulteel of Flete whose son John Crocker Bulteel acquired them in 1801; the latter became the first Master of the Dartmoor Hunt in 1827.

The Dartmoor National Park Committee was approached by a sub-committee of the Hunt in 1954 so that the Hunters' Stone could be re-sited further from the road which was then servicing the construction of the Avon Dam. The Committee allocated £25 for the job to be carried out.

2 Brent Moor House

The ruins of Brent Moor House are all that remain of the Meynell family residence built in the nineteenth century. The Meynells' estate of 3000 acres (1214 ha) stretched far over the southern moors. Attempts were made to enclose some of the moor but local commoners objected.

Mohun Harris subsequently used the building as a hunting-lodge and it was during this time that the rhododendrons which now adorn the valley here were planted. At the turn of the century the house was leased to Rear Admiral John Tuke who was at that time Captain of the Dockyard at Devonport,

Plymouth. Before the Second World War it became a Youth Hostel but apparently was not successful as such—such a place today, no doubt, would be. From late 1954 until 1957 it was used as a dormitory for the Water Board workers engaged in the construction of the Avon Dam. It then lay empty for ten years and was vandalized and, in 1968, the Royal Marines blew up what was left.

3 The Avon Dam Reservoir

The Avon Dam Reservoir was first mooted in 1948 and a public enquiry was held in 1949; the National Park was not to be designated until two years later. The dam took three years to construct and was completed in 1957 for the then South Devon Water Board.

4 Rider's Rings

Rider's Rings is a prehistoric 'village' enclosure. It lies at a height of about 1200 feet (366 m) above sea level and consists of two parts which together comprise about 6 acres (2.4 ha). It is one of the largest known on the moor and contains about thirty-six hut circles (prehistoric round houses) some of which are attached to the inside of the enclosure wall. Here, too, are numerous sub-rectangular 'yards' or stock pens. The two parts of this enclosure suggest an expanding community.

5 Eastern White Barrow

Eastern White Barrow was recorded at the perambulation of the Forest of Dartmoor in 1240 as *Ester Whyteburghe*. This immense prehistoric stone cairn marks a burial dating to about 2000 BC and is about 250 feet (76 m) long and some 36 feet (11 m) high. The 'tower' on the top of the cairn was probably a later addition.

6 Zeal Tor Tramway

Commercial exploitation of peat from Dartmoor began towards the end of the eighteenth century, the product being brought off the moors by packhorse trains. On 11 June 1846 the Duchy of Cornwall (the landowner) granted a licence to L. H. Davy and William Wilkins of Totnes for 'cutting manufacturing and vending peat and peat charcoal.' The licence also allowed the building of a tramway (the Zeal Tor Tramway) for delivering the peat to the treatment works at Shipley Bridge from the ties at Redlake. The venture sadly proved unsuccessful and the factory was closed by 1850.

The tramway returned to partial use in 1872 when the Brent Moor Clay Company purchased all stock and equipment and converted the redundant naphtha works into clay-dries. The tramway was used to carry materials and moorland clay pit workers to and from Shipley Bridge.

LUSTLEIGH CLEAVE

STARTING AND FINISHING
POINT

Trendlebere Down, 2 miles (3.2 km)
north north west of Bovey Tracey on
the Manaton road (191-784793).
From Bovey Tracey continue on the
road passing the main entrance to
Yarner Wood National Nature
Reserve (L) and after going over the
cattle grid follow the road round to L
and park immediately on R on a small
parking area on the edge of the
common.

LENGTH

7 miles (11 km)

ASCENT

Three short climbs all about ⅓ mile
(0.5 km) in length:
ascent 312 ft (95 m) to lower slopes
of Sharpitor;
197 ft (60 m) to Hunter's Tor;
180 ft (55 m) on return to car-park
on Trendlebere Down.

This walk follows public rights of way for its entire length, all being well waymarked. These paths offer beautiful riverside walking including a short detour to Horsham Steps where the river strews its way under and round moss-covered boulders. It follows the side of the Cleave, graced by birch trees, and up along its boldest ridge from which there are spectacular views. Woodland and scrub constitute a great fire risk in the Cleave; guard against all risk of fire.

ROUTE DESCRIPTION (Map 52)

From the car-park walk down the track running alongside the woodland boundary on the R. This is tarmaced in places and is the 'Old Manaton Road', now unsuitable for vehicular use. Where the track levels out we pass part of the Bovey Valley Woodlands National Nature Reserve (R) *(1)*. Continue along the track amongst the oak, holly, hazel, and birch. Ignore a path on the R and go straight on until reaching the Becka Brook. Here, cross over the footbridge (PFS) on R. Turn R and follow path which soon heads L as it contours round the wooded Houndtor Ridge.

We now enter the Bovey Valley. Continue on upstream, keeping the river on the R, for about 1 mile (1.6 km). At the footbridge (R)—comprising two trunks placed end-to-end and with handrail—cross over the river. Follow the bridlepath straight on up the side of the Cleave (PBS 'Lustleigh'). On reaching a path junction, ignore turning on the R, and continue straight on up slope (PBS 'Lustleigh via Hammerslake'). A short steep climb leads to another path junction. Here turn L (PBS 'Foxworthy Bridge') and follow the path down the side of the Cleave keeping Sharpitor Rocks on the R.

On approaching the valley bottom a footpath leads to the L (PFS 'Horsham for Manaton and Water'). A small detour here of 200 yards (183 m) is worth taking to Horsham Steps *(2)*. Retrace steps to continue along the public bridlepath to Foxworthy, passing Foxworthy Mill (L). At Foxworthy Bridge

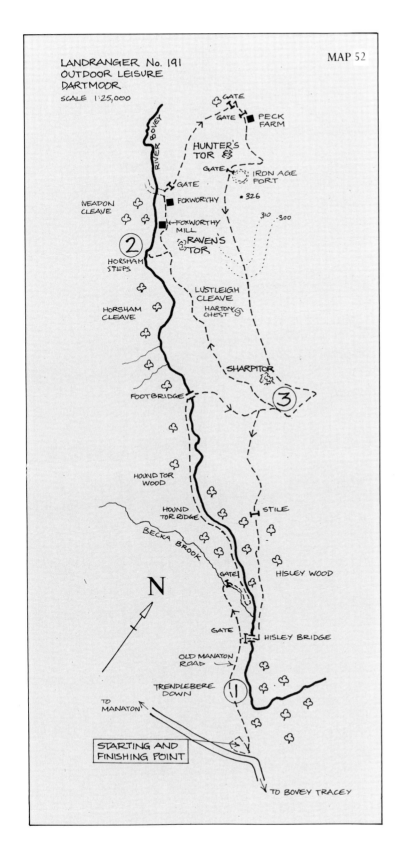

LANDRANGER No. 191
OUTDOOR LEISURE
DARTMOOR
SCALE 1:25,000

MAP 52

GATE
GATE
PECK FARM

HUNTER'S TOR

GATE
IRON AGE FORT

RIVER BOVEY

GATE
FOXWORTHY

NEADON CLEAVE

•326

FOXWORTHY MILL

310 •300

RAVEN'S TOR

②
HORSHAM STEPS

LUSTLEIGH CLEAVE
HARTON CHEST

HORSHAM CLEAVE

SHARPITOR

③

FOOTBRIDGE

HOUND TOR WOOD

HOUND TOR RIDGE

STILE

BECKA BROOK

HISLEY WOOD

N

GATE

GATE
HISLEY BRIDGE

OLD MANATON ROAD

TRENDLEBERE DOWN

①

TO MANATON

STARTING AND FINISHING POINT

TO BOVEY TRACEY

Opposite: *The River Bovey in Lustleigh Cleave.*

bear R following the track (PBS) 'Peck Farm and Road Nr Barnecourt') which swings L in front of dwellings at Foxworthy. Go through a gate and continue on the track until it ends on a farm drive. Go through the gate, turn R and follow the drive up to Peck Farm. Keeping the farmhouse on the L go through a gate (PBS) and walk up the L side of the field. Go L at the top and follow the path which swings half back R to Hunters' Tor.

Go through the gate on reaching Hunter's Tor noticing the subtle low ramparts of the Iron Age fort here on the L. Continue straight on along the ridge, passing the outcrops of Harton Chest (down on R), to Sharpitor (3). Here, keep on the path running alongside the wall (L) and follow down through the wood keeping the tor on the R. Ignore a small path leading to a stile on the L, and near the bottom of the hill, by a gate, go R (PBS 'Clam Bridge/Horsham Steps/Heaven's Gate/Lustleigh and Hisley Bridge'). With Sharpitor Rocks again in view on the R keep to the lower L path and follow down to the next path junction (which we encountered earlier). Continue straight on down the hill (PBS 'Manaton via Water') to the next path junction. Here go L (PBS 'Lustleigh via Pethybridge') and continue straight on. Where the path forks take the R fork for Hisley Bridge. After a short distance go over the stile into the wood and continue on down to the river. At the river turn R and go over the arched packhorse bridge (PBS). Go through the gate and turn L (waymarked 'Nr Holne Brake'). Continue on up the 'Old Manaton Road' to return to the car parking area.

1 *Bovey Valley*
   The Bovey Valley Site of Special Scientific Interest includes most of the Bovey Valley National Nature Reserve and extends for some 646 acres (265 ha). The Site comprises a large area of semi-natural broadleaved woodland, the whole of Lustleigh Cleave and extends up the Becka Brook valley beyond Becka Falls. The River Bovey flows over Dartmoor granite at the north end of the Cleave and on to more easily eroded slates and shales; the junction is marked by rapids.

2 *Horsham Steps*
   Horsham Steps is a curious river crossing-place formed by a number of moss-strewn granite boulders, so close together that the river finds a way underneath them unless in flood.

3 *The Nut Crackers stone*
   On the Ordnance Survey Map Sharpitor has a reference to the Nut Crackers logan stone. This huge rocking stone spectacularly overhung the Cleave until, in 1951, it was pushed off down into the valley below by vandals. In an attempt to heave it back, it fell further and broke into pieces.

Opposite: *The view north from Hunter's Tor.*

189

THE HIGHEST LAND IN SOUTHERN ENGLAND

STARTING AND FINISHING
POINT
Meldon Reservoir, (191-562917)
situated approximately 3 miles (5 km)
to the south west of Okehampton,
highway signposted from the A30.
Construction of the controversial
Okehampton Bypass began in
November 1986; the road is due for
completion in December 1988 and
involves the building of a new slip
road to Meldon. Park in the large car-
park on L approaching the reservoir.
LENGTH
6.5 miles (10 km)
ASCENT
One climb: 2 miles (3 km), ascent
1145 ft (349 m) to Yes Tor.

The walk crosses Meldon dam and follows the West Okement downstream to an area of considerable interest for its industrial archaeology and for its geology. It follows the beautiful Red-a-ven Brook upstream to the lower slopes of Yes Tor and then crosses Dartmoor's highest land to the timeless outcrop of Black Tor.

This walk must not be attempted in poor weather—visibility on the moors can fall rapidly and it may be difficult to find your way back. The walk also enters the Okehampton Firing Range; firing times must be checked.

ROUTE DESCRIPTION (Map 53)

From the landscaped car-park and picnic area, owned by the National Park Authority, pass the toilet block (information board here) and go through the gate. Turn L and follow the lane to the dam (PBS 'Bridlepath to the moor'). Cross over the massive concrete dam *(1)* which impounds the steep-sided valley of the West Okement River. From the dam are dramatic views over the reservoir where Homerton Hill drops beneath the water's edge on its south eastern side. Downstream can be seen the currently worked British Rail's Meldon Quarry (which supplies some 2000 tons of ballast a day), as well as smaller abandoned ones; the massive iron structure of the now unused Meldon viaduct provides an imposing backdrop. Go through the gates at the far end of the dam and turn immediately L through another gate; follow the steps down to the base of the dam.

Walk downstream from the dam on the river's R bank. Cross over the Red-a-ven Brook near to its confluence with the West Okement River. After the Brook carry on straight ahead; do not follow the track round to the R. After some 50 yards (45 m) turn L to cross over the long narrow wooden footbridge which spans the West Okement; a drowned limestone quarry lies opposite *(2)*. Retrace your steps over the bridge and go L along a

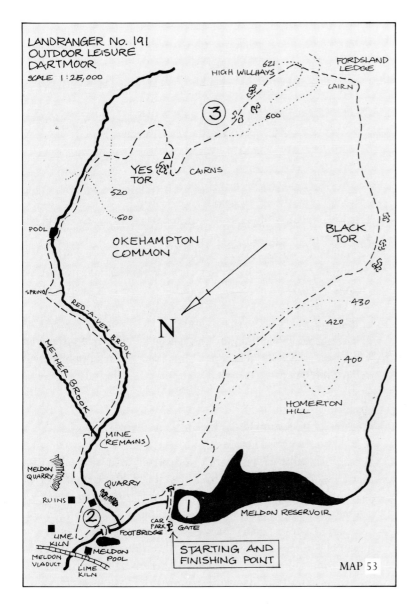

path skirting the edge of the partially grassed-over spoil heaps (on R). Keeping the river on the L, follow the track down towards the viaduct passing a small disused building on the L. Stop by the telegraph pole and ahead lies the restored remains of a large lime kiln—well worth a visit. Retrace steps to the telegraph pole and follow the path round (half L) and head for the large and gaping disused quarry. Keep this quarry on the opposite side of the Red-a-ven Brook; go up the valley passing a massive walled structure and just beyond a smaller non-working quarry on the L.

Follow the track upstream, with the river to the R, passing numerous small waterfalls and pools. At the Range Noticeboard walk down to the river (on R). Here are the remains of an old mine. Return upslope to the Noticeboard and cross the stream (the Mether Brook) and continue straight on keeping two small isolated hawthorn trees to the L. Where a very steep-sided valley known as Sniper's Gully (on R) joins the Red-a-ven Brook, follow the Red-a-ven round to the L. Soon the valley closes in on us. The path becomes ill-defined in places but stay close to the river. The valley soon opens out and a stream issues from a spring ahead, upslope on the L. Turn half L to skirt above the spring, to avoid very boggy ground, and then continue half R to rejoin the riverbank near Yes Tor Ford. Do not cross the river here but continue upstream heading for a series of falls.

The valley begins to get much steeper. Keep the large gully of a redundant military target railway on your L and climb to the small dam and overspill which impound the Red-a-ven Brook forming a small, but deep, pool. This was constructed before the turn of the century to augment Okehampton's water supply. Taking care, we need to cross the river here. Go on upstream, now with the river on the L. Nearing the river's source, the Red-a-ven Brook becomes more of a stream although during wet weather it can become quite violent. The route from the pool can be boggy; the drier ground is close to the river. On reaching a low bluff on the R, after West Mill Tor is to three-quarters L, go R and above the bluff for Yes Tor summit; on a clear day a Range mast and OS Triangulation Point are visible. The route to the Tor encounters a massive clitter slope and it is best to avoid a scramble by following round to the L to ascend the final leg to the Tor's summit. The Tor is worthy of exploration; a ruined prehistoric stone cairn lies on its north-west side. An OS Triangulation Point and the unfortunately-sited military paraphernalia of lookout hut, stable and range pole (although a potentially useful guide if caught in a mist here as the wires rattle in a wind) and wide, heavily-eroded tracks distort a sense of wilderness, unless the soul and mind can overlook such things. The views are extensive—east Cornwall, north and east Devon and Somerset, and much of the northern moors of Dartmoor can be panned.

Walk straight along (due south) the ridge top to the much smaller outcrops—in size, but not height above sea level—of High Willhays (3). Standing on the top of the southernmost pile which terminates the ridge top look to three-quarters R in the direction of the distant, brooding, Great Links Tor; head along a track to the military lookout hut and stable on Fordsland Ledge. Much of Dartmoor's wildest scenery lies before us. Turn R at the lookout hut and pass a prehistoric cairn. Continue in the same direction, bearing slightly to the L, and head down the

Meldon Reservoir.

grass and heather slope to the three granite piles comprising Black Tor.

Aim for the first (southernmost) pile. Keep to the little-used paths, passing a Range Noticeboard on approach, to avoid boggy ground. Continue straight on—to the middle pile with its extensive clitter slopes. Make for the final outcrop and continue half R for an obvious unmetalled vehicle track running over Longstone Hill. Go along this track until Meldon Reservoir comes into view and cut down the slope (half L) for the dam and car-park.

1 *Meldon Reservoir*

The West Okement Valley has been dramatically plugged by the creation of Meldon Reservoir. First mooted in 1962 the consultation process proved to be a long drawn-out saga with the National Park Committee and local and national amenity societies fighting to save what was without doubt an outstanding valley.

The dam is 660 feet (201 m) long and 144 feet (44 m) high and cost £1.6 million to build. The reservoir thus created covers an area of 57 acres (23 ha), its maximum depth of water is 132 feet (40 m) and it has a maximum capacity of 680 million gallons (over 3000 million litres). Water from here is supplied to a population of 200,000 in an area extending from Tavistock in the south to Bideford in the north.

2 *Meldon Pool*

The geology of the Meldon area is extremely complex and

superimposed onto this is a confusing history of past industrial activity which exploited the rock and mineral resources found.

Meldon Pool is 130 feet (40 m) deep and occupies an old limestone quarry. The limited outcrops of limestone in the area were important for producing lime for agricultural purposes in the eighteenth and nineteenth centuries. Near the pool are two limekilns and the one on the river's right

bank was consolidated by the National Park Authority in 1984; this kiln dates from the eighteenth century and is one of the oldest known on Dartmoor.

Up the Red-a-ven Brook, with Yes Tor on the right.

3 *High Willhays*

At some 2038 ft (621 m) above sea level, High Willhays is the highest land in England south of Kinder Scout (2088 ft, 636 m) in the Peak District, some 250 miles (402 km) away.

2.34

NORSWORTHY BRIDGE—EYLESBARROW—DITSWORTHY WARREN—SHEEPSTOR

STARTING AND FINISHING POINT

Norsworthy Bridge at north east end of Burrator Reservoir (202-568693). Take B3212 Yelverton to Princetown road and at Dousland, on approach from Yelverton, go R following highway signs for Burrator and Sheepstor. At Burrator Dam continue straight on for 1½ miles (2.5 km) to Norsworthy Bridge. Car-parking area here on both sides of the road beyond the bridge, 10 miles (16 km) due north west of Plymouth.

LENGTH

7½ miles (12 km)

ASCENT

Three climbs: ⅓ mile (0.6 km), ascent 341 ft (104 m) to Down Tor; ¾ mile (1.2 km), ascent 259 ft (79 m) to Eylesbarrow; ½ mile (0.75 km), ascent 233 ft (71 m) to Sheeps Tor summit.

This area of south west Dartmoor contains some of the National Park's most beautiful scenery and is dominated by the huge pile of Sheeps Tor. South-west Dartmoor also contains a rich variety of antiquities embraced by these wild settings. Included on the route are the remains of our past, spanning some 3500 years. The route also passes Ditsworthy Warren—a commercial rabbit warren which closed in the mid-1950s.

ROUTE DESCRIPTION (Maps 54, 55)

With Norsworthy Bridge, spanning the River Meavy, on the L continue along the road in the direction of Sheepstor going over the small road bridge which crosses the Narrator Brook. Within a few yards the road begins to bear half R. Here, leave the road and continue straight ahead along the walled lane (with forest edge on the R). Pass the remains of Middleworth Farm on the R *(1)*; Middleworth Tor can be seen rising above the trees on the L. On reaching the ruins of the farm settlement at Deancombe, pass the first group of buildings which date from medieval times and before reaching the nineteenth-century remains go L up a rugged tree-lined path, next to an old mine adit. Continue on up passing a sheep pen and go through a gate directly ahead which leads onto the open moor. Follow the path straight up for a short distance, then bear half L for the summit of Down Tor.

From Down Tor go R through the clitter field on the eastern slope and make for a path running parallel with, and to the L of,

196

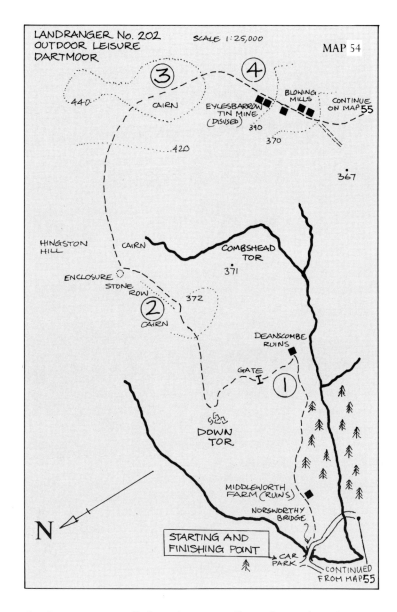

LANDRANGER No. 202
OUTDOOR LEISURE
DARTMOOR

SCALE 1:25,000

MAP 54

the large stone-walled enclosure. Follow the path uphill and where the wall bends away to the R continue half L through the clitter to the crest of this hill. Cross the low banked boundary work (a prehistoric reave) near a cairn and head for the retaining circle and single stone row on the level plain of Hingston Hill *(2)*. Follow the row to the furthest end and continue half L for a circular enclosure and from here go straight on to the cairn, a massive heap of stones. From the cairn continue straight on, keeping the tinners' gullies on the R. At the head of these workings go half R and ascend the hill to the summit of Eylesbarrow *(3)*.

At the PCWW 1917 bondstone, situated between two

prehistoric cairns, continue straight on along a path which drops down to the ruins of Eylesbarrow Tin Mine *(4)* in the direction of the distant china clay spoil heaps.

On approach bear half L and head for the furthest building backdropped by Higher Hartor Tor. Some shafts at Eylesbarrow are only partly filled in and care should be taken when exploring the area. Turn R onto the track and follow down passing the foundations of former blowing mills and on the R a line of granite flat-rod supports. Continue on the track passing an isolated substantial wall, being part of a blowing mill, L and after some 200 yards (219 m) another track leads off to half L. Follow this down to the ruined smelting house.

Follow this track beyond the smelting house to the ford, cross over the Drizzlecombe and contour round to the R in the direction of the hillside outcrop of Shavercombe Tor. Make for Drizzlecombe prehistoric stone rows and the huge cairn known as Giant's Basin *(5)*. Follow the rows down to the last menhir. Continue on in the same direction heading for a group of Scots Pine on the skyline to the L of Eastern Tor to pick a track leading to Ditsworthy Warren *(6)*. Pass the kennel enclosure and house (L) at Ditsworthy Warren and, noticing the pillow mounds ahead, bear immediately R to follow Edward's Path contouring the lower slopes of Eastern Tor; keep Gutter Mire down to the L. On reaching a clump of pine trees go through the gate, passing the Scouts Hut on the R. Go through another gate and turn R onto the track and follow for some 150 yards (137 m). After crossing the leat go L and follow the line, but not the bank so as to prevent erosion, of this watercourse. Keep the leat on the L until two PCWW 1917 bondstones are reached. Here, cross over the leat L, picking the spot that will not disturb the leat banks. Continue straight on, in the direction of Yellowmead Farm. On approaching the enclosure wall bear half R to Yellowmead Stone Circle *(7)*.

The leat further on from here is too wide to cross and it is necessary to retrace steps back to the bondstones. Cross the leat once more and bear L to follow the leat uphill. Where the leat swings abruptly to the L, continue half L to the summit of Sheeps Tor *(8)*. Follow the summit ridge northwards (L) then bear R back down the slope and, half way down, go left heading for Narrator Plantation. Follow the beech-topped wall to the L down to a hunt gate. Go through the gate and on the R are the ruins of Narrator Farm, evacuated and demolished after the building of Burrator Reservoir. Follow the bridlepath half L, between two granite gateposts and on reaching the road go R and follow for about ½ mile (0.8 km) to return to Norsworthy Bridge.

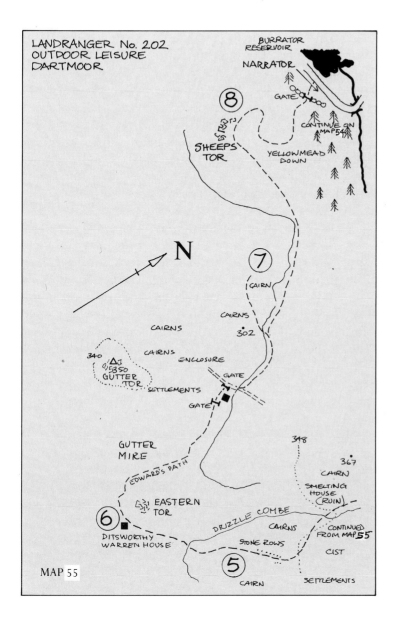

LANDRANGER No. 202
OUTDOOR LEISURE
DARTMOOR

BURRATOR
RESERVOIR

NARRATOR

GATE

⑧

CONTINUE ON
MAP 54

SHEEPS
TOR

YELLOWMEAD
DOWN

N

⑦

CAIRN

CAIRNS

CAIRNS
302

340
△
5350
GUTTER
TOR

CAIRNS

ENCLOSURE

GATE

GATE

SETTLEMENTS

GUTTER
MIRE

EDWARD'S PATH

348

367
CAIRN

SMELTING
HOUSE
(RUIN)

⑥
DITSWORTHY
WARREN HOUSE

EASTERN
TOR

DRIZZLE COMBE

CAIRNS

CONTINUED
FROM MAP 55

STONE ROWS

CIST

⑤

CAIRN

SETTLEMENTS

MAP 55

1   Abandoned farms

Middleworth, Deancombe and Narrator farms, along with about eight others, were evacuated and demolished sometime following the completion of the Burrator Reservoir in 1895 and before its subsequent enlargement in 1928. At Middleworth the dwelling house has almost disappeared following the farm's abandonment in about 1915 after a history of some 634 years. A fine barn survives to its full height having an upper floor, though roofless, and bears a date-stone—'ML 1885'—in the top left hand corner of the outside west wall; the initials 'ML' refer to the landowner at that time—Manasseh Lopes.

2 *Hingston Hill*

The prehistoric monuments on Hingston Hill (Down Tor) are evocatively sited. Here a retaining circle measures some 37 feet (11.2 m) across and this entirely encloses a cairn in which a kistvaen, now gone, was centrally placed. Running eastward from this circle and beginning with a stone almost 10 feet (3 m) high is a single stone row—1145 feet (349 m) in length and which terminates at a blockingstone. Just beyond its eastern end is a large stone cairn and to the north-west of this is a large pound. The standing stones which had fallen down were set back up again in the summer of 1894.

3 *Eylesbarrow*

The great dome of Eylesbarrow rises to 1489 feet (454 m) above sea level and the views from it are very extensive and take in much of the blanket bog areas of the south and north moors.

4 *Eylesbarrow Tin Mine*

The remains of Eylesbarrow Tin Mine lie to the north of the River Plym, some 2 miles (3.2 km) from the river's source. Tinners were known to be streaming in the area in the twelfth century and the earliest known mining reference to Eylesbarrow is 1671.

5 *Drizzlecombe and the Giant's Basin*

Certain places on Dartmoor acquired a special sanctity amongst prehistoric peoples and sometime around 2500 BC they were putting up standing stones often associated with small cairns containing stone coffins or kistvaens. Taken as a whole, the prehistoric remains at Drizzlecombe are amongst the finest on Dartmoor. Here three parallel rows are each headed by a ruined grave with a retaining circle and terminated by a large menhir. The south-east menhir stands 14 feet (4 m) high and is the tallest on Dartmoor.

Close to the rows is a massive cairn, known as the Giant's Basin, a great heap of stones, hollowed out, with a diameter of 70 feet (21.3 m). Whether this large burial barrow is contemporary with the rows has not, as yet, been ascertained. Barrows of this size are usually of a later period, somewhere around 2000 BC. Likewise, the settlement groups to the north-east of the rows may be of a later period.

6 *Ditsworthy Warren*

The Norman Conquest in 1066 brought with it the introduction of the rabbit. These soon became a useful source of food and purpose-built warrens arose in many parts of the country including nineteen on Dartmoor. The oldest on Dartmoor was Trowlesworthy in the Plym valley and dates from the thirteenth century. The medieval-founded Dits-

Opposite: *Menhir, Drizzlecombe—the largest standing stone on Dartmoor.*

Ditsworthy Warren House.

worthy Warren originally extended for 230 acres (93 ha) but was enlarged to cover 1100 acres (445 ha) to form the largest of the Dartmoor warrens.

7 *Yellowmead Stone Circle*

Yellowmead prehistoric multiple stone circle dates from the third millenium BC. It was discovered in 1921 after drought conditions indicated buried stones in an area where dense heather had recently been burnt. The fallen stones were uncovered and erected where they lay later that year. The circle has four concentric rings with diameters of about 21, 38, 48 and 65 feet (6.4, 11.6, 14.6 and 20 m).

8 *Sheeps Tor*

The views to and from the massive granite mass of Sheeps Tor are outstanding. On its summit, within the clitter, is the Pixies' Cave—a natural formation which if you discover you should leave a pin or some other offering for good luck. The cave, it is said, offered refuge for a local eminent Royalist during the Civil War.

1.35

DOONE COUNTRY AND BRENDON COMMON

STARTING AND FINISHING
POINT
Exmoor National Park car-park at
Malmsmead (180-793477).
LENGTH
5 miles (8 km)
ASCENT
600 ft (182 m)

A gentle walk with no tough climbs through moorland steeped in the Doone story. After following the Badgworthy (pronounced 'Badgery') Water upstream, the route veers away westwards to high open moorland where the indistinct track may be easily followed in clear weather but can be hard to trace when an Exmoor mist obscures everything except the immediate surroundings. Walkers are therefore advised to take a compass and be confident in its use. There are extensive views from the highest points, so it is best to reserve this walk for a day of good visibility.

ROUTE DESCRIPTION (Map 56)

Leave the car-park at Malmsmead *(1)*, and take the uphill lane heading south signposted 'Fullinscott, Slocombeslade, Tippacott'. Where the lane bears R, enter the gate L, and follow the track signposted 'Public bridlepath to Doone Valley'. The route passes some mature ash trees L and jinks L and R but continues generally south along a well-defined waymarked track. It dips to Badgworthy Water where Cloud Farm is just across the river *(2)*.

Once past Cloud Farm the landscape becomes more open, the track is nearer the river, and there is more rock in evidence. A short distance further on a memorial stone to R. D. Blackmore is passed *(3)*, and then the track enters Yealscombe and Badgworthy Woods where oak and ash thrive.

The stream flowing down Lank Combe *(4)* is crossed by a footbridge in an attractive rocky glen in open woodland, and the path continues along a steep hillside, crossing Withycombe Ridge Water where a wonderful panorama opens out to the south. Across the river here is a stretch of moorland known as Deer Park *(5)*. The path soon reaches the foot of Hoccombe Combe where a prominent beech hedge crosses the foreground view, and where there is some tumbled ground.

Looking down to Malmsmead from near County Gate.

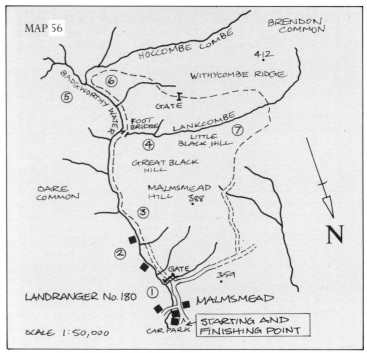

Turn away from Badgworthy Water here and pick up a well-used track heading in a general north-west direction. It at once passes a medieval village site *(6)* and climbs past a ruined cottage, and then the track dips to cross Withycombe Ridge Water and climbs to a gate in a wall. The track is now less distinct as it crosses the featureless plateau of Withycombe Ridge, part of Brendon Common. This is elemental Exmoor, an apparently flat tableland, but broken by countless small valleys. The headwaters of the stream flowing down Lank Combe are crossed at Lankcombe Ford *(7)*, and the walker should now make for the prominent signpost on the skyline to the north, and take the track signposted 'Malmsmead'.

After ½ mile (805 m) or so, at the junction of three tracks, take the L option, and shortly after, L again. Another ford is crossed and the track now leads to the tarmac road about ½ mile (805 m) ahead. Turn R down Post Lane, and Malmsmead is reached in ⅓ mile (535 m).

1 *Malmsmead*
It is here that Jan Ridd brought his bride Lorna, in R. D. Blackmore's celebrated novel *Lorna Doone*. The narrow bridge, the ford, the many horse riders and the red-roofed, whitewashed building now known as Lorna Doone Farm all create an unforgettable image. The Malmsmead Natural History Centre is open midweek in the summer. Shop, café, camp-site and lavatories.

2 *Cloud Farm*
The original house is almost lost among the jumble of stable extensions. The abutments of the old bridge—swept away in the great flood disaster which occurred in 1952—can be seen 25 yards (22 m) upstream from the present footbridge. The Badgworthy Water forms the county boundary between Devon to the west, and Somerset to the east.

3 *The Blackmore Memorial*
A stone beside the path reads:

> To the memory of
> Richard Doddridge Blackmore
> whose novel LORNA DOONE
> extols to all the world the
> joys of Exmoor.

> This stone was placed here by the Lorna Doone
> Centenary Committee 1969

4 *Lank Combe*
The 'slide of water' mentioned by Blackmore is thought to

Badgworthy Water, near Blackmore memorial stone.

have been the one which may be seen up this side valley, but we must remember that *Lorna Doone* is a work of fiction.

5   *The Deer Park*

This was kept as a special reserve for the red deer by Nicholas Snow senior and junior in the last century.

6   *Medieval village site and the ruins of the shepherd's cottage*

The mounds beside the track at the eastern approach to Hoccombe Combe from Badgworthy Water represent a ruined settlement, deserted by 1400. They were woven into his novel *Lorna Doone* by Blackmore as the 'cots' of the Doones. The shepherd's cottage to the west was a much later building, and had a relatively short life.

7   *Lank Combe/Land Combe Hoccombe Combe/Hoccombe Water*

These two pairs of similar names represent different features in the area.

The Horner Valley and Stoke Pero

STARTING AND FINISHING
POINT
National Trust car-park at Horner
(181-897455).
LENGTH
6 miles (9½ km)
ASCENT
1600 ft (490 m)

A sheltered walk through one of Exmoor's finest wooded valleys, entirely in the National Trust's Holnicote (pronounced 'Hunnicut') Estate. The isolated church at Stoke Pero is visited, and the return leg of the excursion is more open, with fine views to Porlock Bay.

Route Description (Map 57)

Leave the car-park at Horner by the way you drove in, turn L, and after 35 yards (32 m) turn R along a short path and cross a narrow stone packhorse bridge over the Horner Water *(1)*. Turn R, and L after 10 yards (9 m) up a steeply climbing path known as Cat's Scramble *(2)* which soon ascends more gently. The woods are initially of oak and beech with an under-storey of holly, and are sufficiently open for bracken to grow. The path, still gradually rising, passes round a small combe with views across to the return path across the valley. From here on the beech trees are absent. Where a path crosses Cat's Scramble go straight ahead *(3)*.

After passing round a second small combe, the path climbs to a patch of old coppice woodland *(4)*. The nests of wood ants are prominent here. At the top of a spur, ignore paths to the L and R and carry straight on. The path descends slightly, bearing R, then ascends again. Here the character of the woodland changes. The oaks are deformed and contorted *(5)*. A path comes in from the R, but may be ignored, and shortly after at an X junction bear L along the contours instead of carrying on uphill. This is Granny's Ride, and should be followed for some distance. Shortly after passing the site of some isolated storm damage a signposted cross path is met. Continue along Granny's Ride. The path narrows and drops steeply to a forestry track. Use this track to carry on down to the Horner Water which should be crossed by a footbridge.

A PFS on the R (south) bank indicates 'Stoke Pero' and this

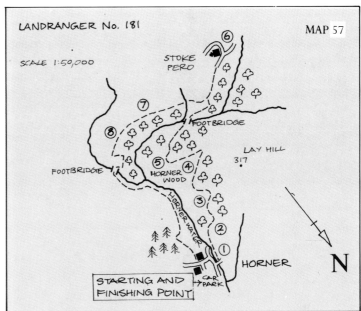

LANDRANGER No. 181

SCALE 1:50,000

MAP 57

STOKE PERO

FOOTBRIDGE

LAY HILL
317

FOOTBRIDGE

HORNER WOOD

HORNER WATER

HORNER

STARTING AND FINISHING POINT

CAR PARK

N

path should now be followed uphill. A path going off to the L 150 yards (137 m) from the bottom should be ignored, likewise another PFS near the top indicates the return route, and can be ignored for the present. The path enters a field and passes into a lane which is followed to a road by a small farm. This is Stoke Pero, and the farm is the only habitation near the church which is 50 yards (45 m) up the road *(6)*.

Return to the PFS in the woods, and take the path R marked 'Webber's Post' ignoring a gate straight ahead. Go steeply down for a short distance, ignoring a path going straight on and turn up R beyond a stream head. At a path junction in a dip, ignore the path going L and continue to follow the straight ahead path. It now emerges from the woods onto a bracken slope and levels out by a seat and some specimen conifers at Cloutsham Ball *(7)*. This is a fine viewpoint.

Beyond the seat take the R path at a fork. At a T-junction, turn L. A deep valley is in front down which flows the East Water. As you descend look out for large pollarded oaks *(8)*. Rejoin the other path, and at once there is another path junction. Follow the Nature Trail signs R. The path descends steeply, and the stream should be crossed by a footbridge.

Now take the path going downstream on the R bank, ignoring a steep path climbing to Webber's Post. At Nature Trail marker no. 7 take the path signposted 'Windsor Walk to Horner'. At cross paths, carry on contouring. Just beyond a signpost reading 'Webber's Post and Windsor Path' another signpost is found in the Scots pines pointing to 'Horner'. Go

Previous page and above: *Horner Water . . . a rich and varied habitat.*

down here, along a pleasant open path. The path gets steeper, passes through a gate and reaches the road just south of Horner. Turn L and the village is soon reached.

1 *Packhorse bridge*
There are several of these narrow, humped-backed bridges in the area. They are probably not more than 250 years old.

2 *Cat's Scramble*
The Acland family gave names to some of the walks and rides on their estate. Cat's Scramble may have been named after an agile pony called 'the Cat' ridden by Lady Acland in the 1870s.
Acland in the 1870s.

3 *Holed oak*
Just before reaching this path junction look L to see the oak with, apparently, a large hole through the trunk. It is likely that, when a young tree, two branches fused together.

4 *Coppice woodland*
Coppicing is a form of woodland management rarely practised in the late twentieth century. At intervals of between ten and twenty years—depending on the market, the need for a cash crop, and the size of timber required—the trees were cut to within 1 foot (½ m) of the ground, and the material sold for a variety of purposes: pit props, fencing, firewood, charcoal and bark for tanning.

5 *Deformed oaks*
These trees are probably contorted as they are on a hillside exposed to the south-west wind. As young trees their twigs were repeatedly torn off and their trunks buffetted by gales.

6 *Stoke Pero church*
The highest church on Exmoor at 1013 feet (307 m). One building, Church Farm, shares its lonely position, but just over 100 years ago twelve cottages stood nearby. Ten farms are scattered around the far-flung parish. The church was rebuilt in 1897, and inside the building is a photograph of Zulu, the donkey which pulled the timber for the new roof up from Porlock.

7 *Cloutsham Ball*
The specimen conifers were planted by the Aclands in the last century.

8 *Pollarded oaks*
Like coppicing (see Note 4 above) pollarding was a system of woodland management rarely practised now. Trees were cut back to within several feet of ground level, probably above the browse-line of red deer, and the branches used for a variety of purposes. The resulting tree is known as a pollard.

2.37

WATERSMEET

STARTING AND FINISHING
POINT
National Trust car-park and picnic
site just inside the Combe Park Hotel
grounds, near Hillsford Bridge (180-
740477).
LENGTH
7 miles (11.2 km)
ASCENT
1200 ft (365.7 m)

A figure-of-eight walk to discover the wooded valleys and breezy uplands of the National Trust's Watersmeet Estate. There are several opportunities for refreshments 'in the season'.

ROUTE DESCRIPTION (Map 58)

Leave the car-park and picnic site by heading for Hillsford Bridge, and walk up the grass verge beside the A39 behind the AA point. Where it tapers, keep to the road edge and make for the National Trust sign 'Watersmeet' 50 yards (45.7 m) ahead. Pass up a pleasant grassy track and enter a gate. These are beautiful, mostly oak, woods, and like so much of the valley woodlands of Exmoor were once managed on the coppice system *(1)*.

Where the path levels out a beautiful view unfolds. Spurs and valleys are complicatedly interwoven. Ignore a PFS by a seat pointing to 'Watersmeet', and carry on, likewise ignoring a PFS pointing L to 'East Lyn'. The views now encompass Lynton and Lynmouth with the Bristol Channel beyond. At an acute path

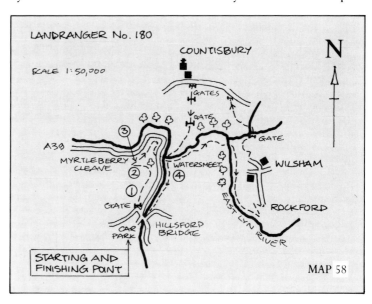

junction R, descend the steep path heading for Watersmeet. Note Butter Hill and Countisbury church *(2)* on the hilltop ahead before losing height. An Iron Age earthwork will be passed through on the open ground before re-entering the woodland *(3)*, then the path hurries down to the road, the A39, which must be crossed to the small National Trust staff car-park opposite. Do exercise care here, as the crossing is on a corner which is almost blind for traffic coming up the road.

The path descends to Watersmeet. Cross the first of two footbridges, over the Hoar Oak Water, but turn up the riverbank of the second river, the East Lyn, instead of crossing the second footbridge *(4)*.

So, walk up the L bank of the East Lyn river, passing the gaping mouth of a short mining adit after a few yards *(5)*. About 400 yards (364 m) upstream are the restored remains of a lime kiln *(6)* with a small quarry nearby. Another 400 yards (364 m) or so upstream take the L fork at a path junction, and cross Ash Bridge when you reach it *(7)*. Turn R on the R bank, and walk up the valley for about 1 mile (1.6 km). Opposite Rockford Cottage—a small café—turn up L at a PFS 'Wilsham Countisbury'. The path zigzags up and turns L along a walled track. The path is waymarked with yellow paint. At Wilsham keep the house with four dormers on your L and follow a broad grassy track northwards.

At an iron gate, turn half R, go down and up into a combe. The path slants up and around a moorland slope and reaches the A39 by an iron gate. Turn L along this busy road, exercising great care, for about 300 yards (274.3 m) when you should turn L into a lane signposted 'Watersmeet'. (This is just behind the Exmoor Sandpiper Inn, formerly the Blue Ball Inn and the Blue Boar Inn.

Follow this gated lane, entering a field at the end and keeping about 25 yards (22.8 m) from the L hedge and aiming for a spur ahead. Note the opposite hillside; this was traversed earlier in the walk. The foot of the field is vacated by a hunting gate, and here there is a PFS sign pointing four ways, and a seat. Go straight ahead, along an attractive grassy spur. The path heading for 'Countisbury' is Winston's Path *(8)*. The path drops off the end of the spur down through the woods, and after the second hairpin bend look out for a sign R marked 'Viewpoint only'. This goes about 45 yards (41 m) through the trees to the top of a rocky buttress overlooking the East Lyn, but do not leave the path or take risks as the drop is considerable.

East Lyn river and Watersmeet House.

Watersmeet—leaf, light and water.

The downhill path reaches the riverside just upstream from Watersmeet House—another refreshment chance. Cross the East Lyn, but instead of going over the Hoar Oak Water, ascend the steps opposite the National Trust money box, turn R at the top signposted 'Hillsford Bridge' and follow the path up to Hillsford Bridge. Do however look out for a short path heading down to the Hoar Oak Water R after 300 yards (274.3 m) from the top of the steps. This leads to a two-stage waterfall viewpoint, and photographers will find it worth seeing.

At Hillsford Bridge, cross the road, cross the bridge, and turn L into the car-park.

1 *Coppice woodland*
See note 4 of 'The Horner Valley and Stoke Pero' walk (page 219).

2 *Butter Hill and Countisbury*
Butter Hill rises to 993 feet, and is crowned by a long-disused signal station, now adapted to modern communications. Countisbury church has the most dramatic situation and inside there is an unusual classical pediment in the chancel arch.

3 *Myrtleberry North earthworks*
A univallate (one-banked) enclosure of about 1 acre (0.4 hectares) with an outwork to the south-west.

4 *Watersmeet House*
Built by the Halliday family about 1830 as a fishing and shooting lodge, it now accommodates a National Trust café and shop. There are lavatories round the back.

5 *Mining adit*
An attempt to find iron ore. An adit is a horizontal shaft. Not much ore was found, hence the short tunnel.

6 *Lime kiln and quarry*
The local soil is acid, but could be sweetened by the addition of lime. Limestone was brought to Lynmouth from South Wales by coasting craft and brought up here by packhorses. Locally-produced charcoal was used in the firing. The small quarry is where the stone came from to build Watersmeet House.

7 *Ash Bridge*
This bridge was built in 1983 by a Manpower Services Commission team.

8 *Winston's Path*
This path is named after Winston Singleton, the National Trust warden who created it.

APPENDICES

Access for the Walker

It is important to realize at the outset that the designation of a National Park does not change the ownership of land within it in any way. In the case of the North York Moors National Park, for example, only 2% of the land area is owned by the Park Authority, compared to the 76.5% of the land which is privately owned. The laws of access and trespass apply just as much to areas of private land within a National Park as to those outside the boundaries.

The National Parks and Access to the Countryside Act of 1949 required County Councils in England and Wales to prepare maps which showed all paths over which the public had a right to walk. The final form of the map is referred to as a definitive map and copies are held at the offices of the County Council and District Council and sometimes by the Community Council concerned. Paths can only be diverted or deleted from a definitive map by the raising of a Division Order or an Extinguishment Order respectively. The paths are classified as either footpaths (for walkers only) or bridleways (for walkers, horseriders and cyclists). These public rights-of-way were included on the now withdrawn one inch to one mile (1:63 360) Seventh Series, the 1:25 000 Second Series (i.e. Pathfinder), 1:50 000 First and Second Series (i.e. Landranger) and the Outdoor Leisure maps.

NATIONAL TRUST AREAS

Currently the National Trust owns 1% of the area of the National Park. The Trust's policy is to give free access at all times to its open spaces.

However, there cannot be unrestricted access to tenanted farms, young plantations and woods, or certain nature reserves where the preservation of rare flora and fauna is paramount.

FORESTRY COMMISSION FORESTS

The Commission allows the public access wherever possible throughout its forest, but it should be emphasized that some of the routes described in this book use permissive paths and not rights-of-way. Forestry operations occur throughout the forests and walkers should keep clear of any working sites and obey any working notices. Always behave in a sensible manner and cause no damage.

PERMISSIVE PATHS

Permissive paths can take the form of either entirely new routes or alternatives to existing paths. In the latter instance, a right-of-way through the middle of a crop field may be supplemented by a permissive path which follows the field boundary, with signs encouraging walkers to follow the new route. Permissive paths are often the result of negotiation between the National Park Authority and local landowners. Often, after an experimental period of use, the NPA will apply for a former right-of-way to be diverted to follow the route of the new permissive path.

Ordnance Survey are now beginning to show permissive paths on the metric editions of the 1:25 000 Outdoor Leisure maps.

Safety

The routes described in this guide vary considerably in both length and difficulty. Some of the easy walks should, with reasonable care, be safe at any time of the year and in almost any weather conditions; the more difficult walks on the other hand, using the high moorland cross-country routes, can be arduous in bad weather. These should be undertaken in winter only by groups of well-equipped and experienced walkers.

It cannot be emphasized too strongly that weather conditions can change very rapidly. What is a drizzle in a valley could be a blizzard on the moor top. Select clothing and equipment for the worst weather you may encounter. Two competent rescue teams are available by police call-out. If you meet with an accident, either to one of your own party or by discovering someone else injured, give what First Aid you are capable of administering. If necessary, shelter the casualty. Write down the grid reference of the incident, and then locate the nearest village or telephone. Ideally two people should go for assistance, leaving someone behind with the casualty, but obviously the decision will be determined by the number in the party.

The golden rules for safety in mountain and moorland areas are:

DO

Carry appropriate clothing and equipment, all of which should be in sound condition.

Carry the correct map and a compass and be practised in their use.

Leave a note of your intended route (and keep to it!).

Report your return as soon as possible.

Keep warm, but not overwarm, at all times.

Eat nourishing foods and rest at regular intervals. Avoid becoming exhausted.

Know First Aid and the correct procedure in case of accidents or illness.

Obtain a weather forecast before you start. Check the local telephone directory under Weatherline.

Keep together if walking in a group; place a strong walker at the back to assist stragglers.

DO NOT

Go out on your own unless you are experienced; four is a good number for a party.

Leave any member of the party behind.

Climb sea cliffs or crags without experience.

Attempt routes which are beyond your skill and experience.

Walk on the cliff-top paths at night; allow plenty of time to clear the cliffs.

A booklet, *Safety on Mountains,* is published by the British Mountaineering Council, Crawford House, Precinct Centre, Booth Street East, Manchester M13 9RZ.

Giving a Grid Reference

Giving a grid reference is an excellent way of 'pin-pointing' a feature such as a church or mountain summit, on an Ordnance Survey map.

Grid lines, which are used for this purpose, are shown on the 1:25 000 Pathfinder, 1:25 000 Outdoor Leisure and 1:50 000 Landranger maps produced by the Ordnance Survey; these are the maps most commonly used by walkers. Grid lines are the thin blue lines one kilometre apart going horizontally and vertically across the map producing a network of small squares. Each line, whether vertical or horizontal, is given a number from 00 to 99, with the sequence repeating itself every 100 lines. The 00 lines are slightly thicker than the others, thus producing large squares with sides made up of 100 small squares and thus representing 100 kilometres. Each of these large squares is identified by two letters. The entire network of lines covering the British Isles, excluding Ireland, is called the National Grid.

FIGURE 3 Giving a grid reference

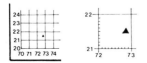

This shows a corner of an Ordnance Survey 1:50 000 Landranger map which contains a Youth Hostel. Using this map the method of determining a grid reference is as follows:

Step 1.
Holding the map in the normal upright position, note the number of the 'vertical' grid line to the left of the hostel. This is 72.
Step 2.
Now imagine that the space between this grid line and the adjacent one to the right of the hostel is divided into ten equal divisions (the diagram on the right does this for you). Estimate the number of these 'tenths' that the hostel lies to the right of the left-hand grid line. This is 8. Add this to the number found in Step 1 to make 728.
Step 3.
Note the number of the grid line below the hostel and add it to the number obtained above. This is 21, so that the number becomes 72821.
Step 4.
Repeat Step 2 for the space containing the hostel, but now in a vertical direction. The final number to be added is 5, making 728215. This is called a six figure grid reference. This, coupled with the number or name of the appropriate Landranger or Outdoor Leisure map, will enable the Youth Hostel to be found.

A full grid reference will also include the identification of the appropriate 100 kilometre square of the National Grid; for example SD 728215. This information is given in the margin of each map.

Countryside Access Charter

YOUR RIGHTS OF WAY ARE

Public footpaths—on foot only. Sometimes waymarked in yellow

Bridleways—on foot, horseback and pedal cycle. Sometimes waymarked in blue

Byways (usually old roads), most 'Roads Used as Public Paths' and, of course, public roads—all traffic

Use maps, signs and waymark. Ordnance Survey Pathfinder and Landranger maps show most public rights-of-way.

ON RIGHTS OF WAY YOU CAN

Take a pram, pushchair or wheelchair if practicable

Take a dog (on a lead or under close control)

Take a short route round an illegal obstruction or remove it sufficiently to get past.

YOU HAVE A RIGHT TO GO FOR RECREATION TO

Public parks and open spaces—on foot

Most commons near older towns and cities—on foot and sometimes on horseback

Private land where the owner has a formal agreement with the local authority.

IN ADDITION YOU CAN USE BY LOCAL OR ESTABLISHED CUSTOM OR CONSENT, BUT ASK FOR ADVICE IF YOU ARE UNSURE

Many areas of open country like moorland, fell and coastal areas, especially those of the National Trust, and some commons

Some woods and forests, especially those owned by the Forestry Commission

Country Parks and picnic sites

Most beaches

Canal towpaths

Some private paths and tracks. Consent sometimes extends to riding horses and pedal cycles.

FOR YOUR INFORMATION

County councils and London boroughs maintain and record rights-of-way and register commons. Obstructions, dangerous animals, harassment and misleading signs on rights-of-way are illegal and you should report them to the county council

Paths across fields can be ploughed, but must normally be reinstated within two weeks

Landowners can require you to leave land to which you have no right of access

Motor vehicles are normally permitted only on roads, byways and some 'Roads used as Public Paths'

Follow any local by-laws.

AND, WHEREVER YOU GO, FOLLOW THE COUNTRY CODE

Enjoy the countryside and respect its life and work

Guard against all risk of fire

Fasten all gates

Keep your dog under close control

Keep to public paths across farmland

Use gates and stiles to cross fences, hedges and walls

Leave livestock, crops and machinery alone

Take your litter home

Help to keep all water clean

Protect wildlife, plants and trees

Take special care on country roads

Make no unnecessary noise.

This charter is for practical guidance in England and Wales only. It was prepared by the Countryside Commission.

Addresses of Useful Organizations

British Mountaineering Council
Crawford House
Booth Street East
Manchester M13 9RS
Manchester (061) 273 5835

British Trust for Conservation Volunteers
36 St Mary's Street
Wallingford
Oxfordshire
Wallingford (0491) 39766

For those who wish to help with countryside conservation, e.g. repairing drystone walls, maintaining footpaths, at weekends or holiday times.

The Camping and Caravanning Club of Great
  Britain and Ireland Ltd
11 Lower Grosvenor Place
London SW1W 0EY
01-828 1012

Council for National Parks
4 Hobart Place
London SW1W 0HY
01-235 0901

Countryside Commission
John Dower House
Crescent Place
Cheltenham
Gloucestershire GL50 3RA
Cheltenham (0242) 521381

Countryside Holidays Association
323 Birch Heys
Cromwell Range
Manchester M14 6HU
061-225 1000

Forestry Commission (Wales)
Victoria House
Victoria Terrace
Aberystwyth
Dyfed SY23 2DG
Aberystwyth (0970) 612367

The Long Distance Walkers Association
Membership Secretary
Lodgefield Cottage
High Street
Flimwell
East Sussex TN5 7PH
Flimwell (058 087) 341

The National Trust
36 Queen Anne's Gate
London SW1H 9AS
01-222 9251

Nature Conservancy Council
Northminster House
Northminster Road
Peterborough
Cambridgeshire PE1 1UA
Peterborough (0753) 40345

Ramblers' Association
1/5 Wandsworth Road
London SW8 2LJ
01-582 6878

Wales Tourist Board
Distribution Centre
Davis Street
Cardiff CF1 2FU
Cardiff (0222) 487387

Youth Hostels Association
Trevelyan House
8 St Stephens Hill
St Albans
Hertfordshire AL1 2DY
St Albans (0727) 55215

INDEX

Page numbers in *italics* refer to illustrations.